# Hearing Ourselves

Other titles in
The Growth and Healing, Pastoral Care
and Counselling series

*To Sister Elizabeth CSF*
*for listening deeply*

*I would like to thank Christine Whitell, Editor of Marshall
Pickering, for her encouragement to turn an inauspicious jumble into
a book; and to Margaret Wellings for her skill in turning a pile of
scrap paper into a manuscript.*

# Hearing Ourselves

*Verena Tschudin*

Marshall Pickering

Marshall Morgan and Scott
Marshall Pickering
34–42 Cleveland Street, London, W1P 5FB, UK

All biblical references are taken from
the Jerusalem Bible.

*British Library CIP Data*

Tschudin, Verena
    Hearing ourselves.
    1. Christian life. Spirituality
    I. Title
    248.4

    ISBN 0–551–018738–9

Text set in Baskerville by Photoprint, Torquay, Devon.
Printed in Great Britain.

# Contents

# Introduction

This is a book about awareness. It is a very small book and awareness is a very big subject. Learning is a life-long experience. I have therefore used words and concepts without explaining them too closely.

By the word soul I mean anything in the inner life. This may seem simplistic in today's world. It is however a much older concept than the many differences propounded in esoteric literature. In trying to bring together the outer and inner into a unity, the simpler the starting point, the better.

I have used the word God almost exclusively throughout, not making a distinction between Father, Son, and Spirit.

I have also posed many questions in the text. These are meant to stimulate the reader to find her or his own best way of answering or responding: of becoming aware what she or he means and understands when using the words 'God' or 'soul'.

I have used many biblical texts, and more than likely left out many more which may seem obvious to readers. May I be forgiven for still only seeing 'through a glass darkly' (1 Cor. 13:12). May it also be a stimulus to the reader to come to other, and newer insights, and use them.

# Listening to the Body

This section concentrates on self-awareness through listening to the body. The body is that which is nearest to us and through which we express who we are.

## Awareness

'In the beginning was the Word' (John 1:1). The Word – not light, or fire, or wind. No, in the beginning was the Word. God did not *think* the world into being, but He spoke. He said, 'let there be light, and dry land, and animals, and mankind'. And they all came into being because they listened to the Word speaking. Their continued existence depends on their awareness of themselves and of God.

Listening is the basic, instinctual activity, but it never happens just for its own sake. God does not speak to hear the sound of His own words in the echo of dead space. The spoken word commands attention and it is only fulfilled when a response is made.

Awareness then, is never an end in itself. It only exists so that more of God, more of love, is created. 'As the rain and the snow come down from the heavens and do not return without watering the earth, making it yield and giving growth to provide seed for the sower and bread for the eating, so the word that goes from my mouth does not return to me empty, without carrying out my will and succeeding in what it was sent to do' (Isa. 55:10–11). By listening and hearing we take part in the cycle of awareness, response and growth.

Listening is very easy in today's world. We are surrounded by sounds everywhere, and with the advent of Walkman cassettes we need never be without our favourite tune or message. But that sort of listening makes us rather deaf, I fear.

From the beginning of history people have preferred to be deaf rather than to listen to what was said and to respond to it. Adam and Eve preferred to go round with fig leaves over themselves rather than to listen to God and His command (Gen. 3:1–13). By covering up their senses and their bodies they removed themselves from that direct, 'naked' relationship with God.

Living is being alive, awake, alert. John Taylor in his book *A Matter of Life and Death*[1] claims that most people are most of the time more dead than alive. He equates aliveness with responsiveness, and deadness with apathy. 'We actually choose to be less alive in order to be less bothered.' Deadness is less hard work than aliveness. It is less difficult to put on the fig leaves every day than to remain naked, listening to God.

Living is something that we need to do actively. It does not just happen. 'I set before you life or death, blessing or curse. Choose life, then.' (Deut. 30:19). Every choice that we make is a sign of life. And every choice we make is based on something that we listened to, perhaps with our ears, but certainly with our understanding.

When we are really alive we are aware of many things: our bodies, surroundings, relationships, thoughts and wishes, actions and the influences we have. Listening is an activity both of the ears and the understanding: we listen to what we can hear – the 'material' – and to what we can only grasp with the mind and the spirit.

For this reason a 'body experience' is not better or worse than a 'spiritual experience'. Sometimes an awareness of God comes through the body, and sometimes a spiritual experience frees us to act in a certain way. Listening gives us the power and freedom to hear what is happening and to respond to it.

Becoming and being aware leads to greater wholeness. This is a wholeness of body, mind, thoughts, relationships, actions or any of the influences around us. One responds to and influences the other.

The aim of this book is to help you to come to a greater awareness. The first step to awareness is listening and hearing what goes on in and around us. When we listen to the Word going forth from the mouth of God we become aware of its message to us, and of the message which we are. We listen to become aware to respond.

## Listening

In both the Old and New Testament people are constantly told, 'Listen!'. Listening seems much more important than seeing. God is not a vision, but the Word. Rabbi Ashkenazi[2] said in an interview, 'We are not the people of the Book as we are called. We are the people of the Word of Him, who have this "word" put into writing in a book'. First of all we listen.

God told His people to listen to him. Moses told them to listen and keep the commandments (Deut. 5:1). The cry of the prophets, one by one, was 'listen to the voice of the Lord' (Jer. 38:20), and the Father says to us of His Son 'Listen to him' (Luke 9:35). As people of the Word, we listen.

Much of what we actually hear we never register at all. It is therefore difficult to discern what it is that we should listen to, and having heard it, how good or true it is. So that we are able to listen carefully and creatively, we need, in a way, to reverse what Adam and Eve did, and establish again that 'naked' relationship with God. We need to take the fig leaves off our senses and learn to commune again with God, each other and all creation in that way in which every word spoken is heard and responded to.

Although listening is instinctual, we need to learn constantly how to do it. That is why it is so difficult. We need to learn *how* to listen again and again, and to listen to new things, new words. If we want to go forward in life we can only do it one step at a time, and each step has its distinctive 'word' which we need to discern.

In listening to ourselves, our environment, other people and God, we hear what the significant steps in our lives are. We discover in them the meaning of our lives. When we find ourselves resisting the need to listen, then the battle begins. Jeremiah (20:9) seemed to have a fire burn in his heart, imprisoned in his bones, when he stopped listening to God and speaking in His name. So we, when we stop listening to God and ourselves, become ill, physically and metaphorically, and also spiritually. To stay well we have to listen.

To divide this listening into different categories or activities as I have done in this book is somewhat arbitrary. When we hear a bird sing we hear not only that bird, but perhaps a word from God. But we are not always in the same way receptive to the differing impacts that these levels of hearing have on us. Writers and theologians down the ages have described the journeys of the soul, and the stages on that journey. Awareness of the body, environment and soul go together, but not always in equal measure. Awareness of the body comes on the whole before awareness of and in the soul. First we have to become aware of who we are. Only later do we become aware of the meaning of that being.

The three divisions of listening I am therefore making may also correspond to three stages of life, and even three ages of life. But we can never listen to only one aspect. To become whole we have to listen to the whole. I hope that by looking at the different parts of awareness separately will be like a jig-saw puzzle, eventually coming together into a whole.

## Body

Most of us take our bodies for granted. They are after all that aspect of ourselves which we know best. From the first day of our lives we were aware of hunger or discomfort, and were able to express this through the body, by crying. We have learnt to be aware particularly of the things which go wrong with our bodies. That is our defence for staying alive.

Awareness of the body is more than just an awareness of the things which have gone wrong with it. Most of us are not aware of how we breathe and walk and swallow. All these things go on automatically most of the time, and so nature has ensured that things essential to survival are made as easy as possible. Yet survival and being alive are not the same thing. In times of crisis we need only a few essential things to survive; for being alive we need a whole range of different strategies, ways, means and possibilities.

One of the first means of becoming aware of the body is through breathing. Most of us use on the whole only the top halves of our lungs for breathing. When we become aware of breathing we also become aware of our back; the rise and fall of the chest and arms, and the tummy.

Breathing is more than just inspiring: it is also 'inspiriting'. Through breathing we take in the spirit, and life. God had breathed into Adam's nostrils 'a breath of life, and thus man became a living being' (Gen. 2:7). Take a few slow, deep breaths, and become aware of the breath of life in your nostrils, your body, your soul.

To become aware of the body is to become aware of its functioning. Most of us spend vast amounts of time grooming, cleaning, beautifying and maintaining ourselves. This generally relates to the outside, the skin part. Do we do enough to be aware of the various internal organs, like the heart, kidneys and gut? My dentist tells me that I have not enough 'tooth awareness' because I don't feel the holes in them. We take our bodies for granted until something goes wrong.

Becoming and being aware of the body also means that we are conscious of the posture we have, the kind of impact we make on others, where we locate our various feelings, where the flow of energy lies, and so on. In the body we are living; through awareness of the body we become alive.

To be aware of a headache is also being aware of the whole world in which headaches function. It is not enough to explain a headache in terms of tension, lack of fresh air, or hunger. We need to see a headache also in terms of ourselves being the headache to ourselves; of how we allow the pain into the head and keep it there and use it for our own ends. What are we saying to ourselves and to the world with a headache? What kind of attention does this pain (do we) need?

To be aware of the body functioning well makes us thankful, and being thankful makes us even more aware of even more things around us. Being thankful makes us alive.

## Health

Through listening to the body we become aware of who we are, what we are, and how we are in the world which surrounds us.

Every newspaper and magazine these days is full of advertisements for this and that product to make us healthier. But is their aim health, or simply the absence of disease; is it life, or simply a prolongation of time on earth? Do these advertisements point towards 'health for all by the year 2000' the aim set by the World Health Organisation, or is it simply a ploy for exploiting our fear of death and dying? What do these terms point to as our response to what we listen to?

Health has been officially defined as 'a state of complete physical, mental and social wellbeing, and not merely the absence of disease or infirmity'.[3] By this definition none of us is 'healthy' because none of us lives in a constant state of complete health, happiness, freedom or riches.

Some people have chosen to live in poverty, but that does not make them unhealthy. Some are mentally ill; some others may merely be 'eccentrics'. Many live with permanent disability, or diseases like diabetes, but they would not describe themselves as ill. Yet others try to convince themselves that they are well when it is obvious that this is far from the truth. I remember Mary, who insisted that there was nothing more the matter with her than old age, and its manifestations of increasing tiredness and clumsiness. When she broke a foot through 'clumsiness' and had to go the hospital for this, it was soon evident that she had disseminated cancer.

What does health mean to each of us? In these days of scarce resources one person's health might mean another person's continued ill-health. As we listen to our bodies, the temples of the spirit, we might also hear the wider issues.

Our health has been entrusted to us like a talent (Matt. 25:14–30). It is not something which we have by right, but something which we must cherish, use and care for. Perhaps, at the end of life, the Master will ask us, what we have done with this talent, this health? Did we use it or abuse it? Did we care for it or pamper it?

Once we listen seriously to the body, and hear what it says to us, we can no longer ignore the issues of health in general, and our own health in particular. As we listen in a new way to unexpected things to do with physical, spiritual and mental health we may find that the view we had so far of health and health-issues will be challenged. Jeremiah became ill when he stopped listening to what he heard inside himself. Today many people suffer from burn-out because they have stopped listening to their inner voice. The body then functions like a machine which is kicked into functioning every morning rather than kissed to new life by the spirit.

### Illness

More than anything else, an illness or accident or time in hospital makes us aware of ourselves. It brings us up with a jolt and makes us take stock.

Illness – from a cold to cancer – means a time of enforced rest and inactivity, giving us a change of pattern. Many people find this devastating. We identify ourselves with doing, controlling, and being in charge. To be done to, controlled, and taken charge of goes against the grain. We rail against the illness, and blame whoever or whatever gave it to us.

Satan is very well aware of the devastating effect of illness. When he saw that Job had not capitulated after all the disasters he had sent on him, he had one more card to play when he met God: 'skin for skin. Stretch out your hand and lay a finger on his bone and flesh; I warrant you, he will curse you to your face' (Job 2:4–55).

Satan knows a person's vulnerable part. People will barter their lives away to save their skin. And the quicker the better. Pills and potions come out to deaden every physical and mental and spiritual pain. We feel that we can't afford to be ill.

A patient in hospital said to me once, 'I was so desperate to find an answer, if possible an easy one. I thought, ah well, it's just a little lump in the elbow and they can just remove it and all will be well'. He had an inkling that something more serious was happening: in fact he had a brain tumour.

Illness is dis-order and dis-ease. For someone to listen to illness is therefore to listen to chaos, to conflict, and to unease. This can be unsettling to the point of leading to depression. To take a pill to feel better, or to be jollied along and cheered up may not be the appropiate care. But like Job 'to go and sit in the ashpit' (Job 2:8) may be more necessary. Even to feel what the ashpit is like may be more relevant. That same patient said, 'But now with the treatment I can't read and I can't rest. In fact, I find it very difficult to be true to myself'.

For the person concerned and for the onlookers, this is a testing time. To admit that it is difficult to be true to oneself can be that moment of insight, that 'I see!' which sheds new light around and gives a person the strength to get up from the ashpit.

When we allow ourselves to hear what an illness has to say to us we will be changed. An illness may not necessarily be changed into health, but it may be changed into wholeness. When we listen to the illness and hear what it has to say to us, it may ask us, like Christ, 'What do you

want me to do for you?(**Matt**.20:32). The awareness of an
illness will eventually bring us to an awareness of our real
need: 'Lord, let us have our sight back' (Matt. 20:33). To
have become ill may be to have become 'blind' in many
ways.

An illness is often the starting point for an inner journey
which we might have avoided. All the things and events
described in this book – and many, many more which could
never be listed nor described – can be the trigger for new
awareness and new responses. Illness is an 'obvious'
trigger, but other things may be more real for someone.
Whatever the trigger, whatever the voice or the word
spoken, we need to take it seriously, and listen to it.

When we are listening, we are first of all listening to
ourselves. What we are hearing is ourselves, and our needs
and wants. We become conscious, awake.

### Mind

The famous phrase, 'Know thyself' written apparently over
the entrance to the temple of Apollo (the god associated
with beauty and prophecy), has caused a lot of controversy
down the ages. Carlyle though that the statement should be
'Know what thou canst work at'. Carlyle was a politician,
and perhaps this is a very apt dictum in politics.

Descartes' notion of 'I think, therefore I am' is another
one of those sayings which are so simple, yet so elusive.
Neither of these statements relates only to the mind, though
for philosophers the mind has often played a major role, to
the detriment of the body.

Listening brings us in touch with another dimension.
Merton[4] reminds us that beyond our consciousness is
Being. This is not an experience of consciousness. It is not a
state of awareness. 'The consciousness of Being is an
immediate experience that goes beyond reflexive awareness.
It is not "consciousness *of*" but *pure consciousness*.'

Listening brings us into an awareness at many levels: our
bodies, our minds or spirits, our souls, and it brings us to
the awareness of Being: of God, of love, of life.

If you are able, close your eyes for a moment, and *think* what you mean by mind, consciousness, being. Stay with the thoughts and images which present themselves. Acknowledge them without judging them.

You may be surprised to find what they say about you, others and God. Surprise into joy and creativity is one of the ways in which the spirit works. Therefore listening is often a surprising activity. The three sayings above about awareness all point in different directions, emphasising the importance which different ages placed on consciousness and the mind. Listening leads us to awareness of ourselves and all that surrounds us. The purpose of hearing ourselves is not an end in itself, but it is a means to an end: to be and become more that which we essentially are already.

## Temperament

Self-awareness and self-knowledge help us to respond to the Word in whatever way we hear that Word speak.

Self-awareness is not something which we acquire overnight. It is a long and often slow process, and essentially never finishes. Sometimes we get a whole packet of insight at once, sometimes just a little glimpse. Certain methods to gain self-knowledge can propel us along the path, and most of us will have used such methods at one time or another. Psychoanalysis is one such way. The various schools of astrology (Western and Eastern) are another widely known way. Schools and courses without number offer their services for various kinds of thought-processes and 'getting in touch with' whatever name we give to that elusive something which constitutes our self, our life.

Down the ages people have been described in terms of different temperaments. Keirsey and Bates[5] have described the Myers-Briggs Type Indicator (a test for determining the psychological type) in clearly understandable form. The following is simply a brief overview of the different temperaments. No one temperament is better than another: we are simply different.

The indicator outlines four pairs of *preferences* by which people express themselves. These are only generalisations, and no-one is definitely in either one category or the other, but life has made us *prefer* one to the other. You may like to consider which preference suits you best.

The first preference is that of the *basic orientation*: people are either *extroverted* or *introverted*. The next two pairs are the so-called *functions*: the perceiving and judging functions. The perceiving functions – the way in which people perceive, or recognise, the world – is either by their *senses* or their *intuition*. Having perceived the world, people then use their judging function to come to grips with it, and they judge the world either by *thinking* about it, or by *feeling* it. Lastly, the *attitude* which people then take to that environment is either in a *judging* (meaning orderly) way, or in a *perceiving* way. Thus a person can be extroverted, sensing, thinking and perceiving; or introverted, intuitive, feeling and judging, or any combination of the four types.

Most of us have a good idea of what we are in the basic orientation: extrovert or introvert. From there on it is often less clear. Ideally we would be not specifically either–or, but be able to use both possibilities in each instance; to be able equally well to function in a sensing and intuitive way, by thinking and by feeling. But for survival most of us have developed a predominance in one or other of these functions.

A small outline of the various aspects of these functions may be helpful here.

An *extroverted* person will get his or her energy from being with other people; an *introverted* person from being alone.

A *sensing* person will on the whole concentrate on what is present; will place faith in facts; will find fantasy difficult; will be realistic, down-to-earth, practical, and will always see that any solution should be workable.

An *intuitive* person will by nature be thinking things up; will be concerned with what may be possible; will be following a hunch; is ingenious; always future-oriented, and will therefore see that any solutions have room for growth and improvement.

A *thinking* person will be very objective and do anything as long as it is reasonable; will be knowledgeable as regards principles, laws, and policies; will therefore be firm, just, and sometimes impersonal; will only agree to solutions as long as they are systematic.

A *feeling* person will usually please; will place value on harmony and humane treatment; will often be 'working with people'; will try to persuade rather than rule and will look for extenuating circumstances in difficulties; will want solutions to be reached by agreement with all concerned.

These are only very broad pointers to some of the characteristics. Nevertheless they can give us a little insight into the type of temperament we have. To have that knowledge can be helpful in realising why we act as we do, and why others act differently from us. This self-knowledge is not an excuse for some specific behaviour, but it can make us more tolerant – of ourselves and others. It can also help us to know what our weak points are, and where we might look to improve them. Self-knowledge is an intellectual understanding of our character; self-awareness is an emotional, feeling insight into the self – the two complement each other.

## The Senses

Our contact with the world and with the things which surround us is through the senses.

The senses are the links between the inner and the outer world, the physical and the metaphorical. We say 'I see' and this has nothing to do with the two physical eyes, but the 'inner eye', that which understands. In this book I am using hearing and listening not only in the physical sense, but also in the metaphorical: the understanding as well as the mechanical reception of tone. Yet we cannot understand unless we have first perceived in the physical and literal sense. We see, hear, smell, taste and touch, and in this way make sense of our surroundings.

Sacks, in his book *A Leg to Stand On*[6] describes how after an accident he nearly despaired of walking properly again.

'And suddenly – into the silence, the silent twittering of frozen images – came music, glorious music, Mendelssohn, *fortissimo*! Life, intoxicating movement! And, as suddenly, without thinking, without intending whatever, I found myself walking, easily, *with* the music.' But Sacks *heard* music, and as he listened to it, he could walk. Listening changed his life.

Saul, on the road to Damascus (Acts 9:1–9) heard a voice. The men with him did too, but saw no one speaking. But Saul listened to the voice – and what a shock it must have been to hear *Jesus* speaking to him – and his life was changed.

The sense of hearing is crucial in our understanding of life. We become aware through listening – with our ears and with our heart. So that we can really become alive we need to understand the *message* of what was said or heard, or implied. The words themselves are merely the conveyors. 'Take care of the sense and the sounds will take care of themselves', said the Duchess to Alice.[7]

Seeing is secondary to hearing in the spiritual way of understanding. Seeing leads so easily to idolatry. The story of Narcissus who looked at himself in the water and fell in love with his own image is salutary. We can see and stay put with what we see. Or we can see and in this way come to a greater understanding of ourselves and of the object which we see. We can look at a sunrise and worry about the day it heralds. We can look at a sunrise and let it awaken in us a sense of belonging with the world, with all things and all people, and with God.

The sense of smell is perhaps the Cinderella among the senses. Yet how much time and money do most of us not spend on enhancing attraction, or destroying bad odours? A person without the sense of smell is almost as much at risk as a person without sight or hearing. Not to find out when a saucepan burns dry, which rose to give as a present, or if the person next to you on a seat is friend or foe, is not only a handicap, but may even be dangerous.

Taste, like all the senses, links inner and outer worlds. We taste bread and wine, and with it we 'taste and see' the goodness of the Lord (Ps. 34:8). Our taste of bread and wine is temporary – but the taste of the goodness of God is profound, and lasting.

I have the privilege of often helping with the distribution of Holy Communion in my church. Sometimes on giving the chalice to a person I can see and feel a deep 'communion' of that person with God. Perhaps that person could not put into words what is happening, but the effect is very powerful and real.

When we listen to our senses, and what they convey to us, we will become aware of a world to which we had perhaps paid little attention. Each sense has its own message, its own word for us. And that word is 'sweeter than honey, even honey that drips from the comb' (Ps. 19:10).

Touching, the last sense is, like the others, a two-edged sword. Used with love, a touch becomes a caress; used with malice, a painful slap. Touch, unlike the other senses, is intimately connected with sensitivity, sensibility, sexuality and sensuality. No wonder that many people are afraid of touching!

'Sensory deprivation' has come to be a recognised phenomenon in many old people, and also in the mentally handicapped. Giving them a cat to look after may not be the whole answer, but it may be one answer.

At this time many of us grapple afresh with our own sexuality because AIDS has come and challenged old habits and viewpoints. Touching, and being touched, is for many of the people infected with AIDS one of the most important aspects of living. To what extent will we be willing to listen to what touch and touching has to say to us? What response will we be willing to make to the demands of this sense?

Ella, from Norway, and Meg had met one summer on holiday on the Continent and had stayed in touch for many years. Then Ella decided to come to England for a holiday. They didn't know if they would get on with each other, and indeed they had some differences. Meg went to the airport with Ella for the return journey. Ella was already in the queue for passport control when suddenly she jumped out, ran towards Meg and dragged her a few feet away. There she looked at Meg, and with her thumb made a cross on Meg's forehead, saying something. Ella explained that this was a blessing which her mother had often used, and she now handed on to Meg. Then she was back in the queue and they lost sight of each other.

Meg felt that cross on her forehead for a long time. But she was aware of the blessing handed on for much longer, and their friendship became a real blessing to each of them.

In the New Testament two women's lives were changed through touch: the woman with the haemorrhage who touched Christ's cloak (Luke 8:44) and Mary, who held on to the risen Jesus as if never to let Him go again. 'Do not cling to me' is the response to her (John 20:17) and she understood the message.

The senses are the go-betweens between physical and spiritual, between material and mental understanding. They bring these two worlds together. Their message, here as everywhere, is to listen: 'something which has existed since the beginning, that we have heard, and we have seen with our own eyes; that we have watched and touched with our hands: the Word, who is life – this is our subject' (1 John 1:1).

## Sexuality

One of the most intimate ways of knowing our bodies is through sexuality. Perhaps more than health and illness, the mind or the senses, sexuality characterises us. Therefore it can also frighten us.

We are sexual beings and we have no choice over the gender we are. This may be why those people who change sex or are transvestites hold such a fascination. Our sexuality, like the colour of our eyes, is determined from the first moment of life.

When we listen to our sexuality, myriads of images come to life. I would first like to look at some of the images which are concerned with gender in general, and then those which are concerned with genitality.

We have heard a lot in recent years about women's liberation. We are becoming aware of one whole side of our being which has often been suppressed, at least in the Western world. It seems that at the moment men are also talking more of being liberated. Liberation here means being able to be ourselves, not confined to stereotypes.

When we listen to ourselves, and particularly to our bodies, we discover untold sources and areas within us which are very personal to us, and characteristic of each one of us. We are unique – we are different. To be able to express this uniqueness takes a lot of courage. And we are not unique if from the first moment of life we are labelled with either a pink or a blue label: just the one or the other, and from then on we are pressured to conform. What does this say to us? What does it all mean to us? It may help us to find our personality, but it may also help us to suppress it.

The freedom which the various liberation movements bring are good and beautiful. But so that these freedoms stay good and don't get abused in other ways, we have to guard them, and care for them. Freedom is not licence to do as we please. Freedom rightly used gives the person next to us as much freedom and right as ourselves.

The way in which most of us express our gender in its most poignant form is through genital contact. We are attracted to the opposite in order that we can fulfil ourselves and the other. In genital contact we give and receive the essence of ourselves. 'Making love' is truly what it says: we create ourselves, our partner, and sometimes also a child in the act of intercourse. In being totally united with another person, and becoming 'one flesh' (Gen. 2:24) we go beyond ourselves both physically and spiritually. So much about God is described in terms of physical love, of union, of ecstasy, and of being lost in the other, that it is not difficult to see how through sexual love we come nearer to God's love.

Precisely because sexual love is so unique and so special,

it is so easily abused. A basic instinct to grab and possess will make us want to possess sexuality too. This reduces not only the sexual act to one of egoism, but at the same time it diminshes the other person concerned. The glory of sexuality is that it is not something which we do, but something which we share. Only when both people concerned are enhanced and affirmed can sexuality really be seen as fulfilling itself.

When we listen to our bodies we hear their urges and desires and needs, and the urge of sexuality may be very strong. What does it mean for us? Where does it lead us? What does it point us to? What does it say about us as a person?

Sexuality is not only joy. It is often very frustrating too. It makes itself felt at the most embarrassing moments and when we are in the most romantic situation we feel like a block of wood. Every ingenious aphrodisiac will not help us then. What does help is not fast talk and persuasion, but listening. Hearing ourselves and particularly hearing the other. What is going on? Many romances have been created in bed, and many romances might be re-created in bed, with patience and love, listening and silence.

I am aware also of the many people I know who have never had penetrative sex. I am thinking in particular of Mark, a severely disabled man, who longed for a 'real' relationship with a woman, but his handicap and upbring-ing had prevented it. And the people, like monks and nuns for instance, who have chosen not to have sexual relation-ships. Such people are not any less fulfilled. Their fulfil-ment is elsewhere. It is us and our stereotyped attitudes who think that they are not 'complete'. Perhaps we think and speak only out of our own 'incompleteness'?

Sexuality, like everything in and of the body is not something which we can classify and judge. We can only use it, and grow through it, and let it be creative.

## 'The glory of God is man fully alive'

The aim of living is not self-awareness, but self-transcendence. Ultimately we are not on this earth for ourselves only, but so that, with others, the Kingdom of God will come.

St Irenaeus of Lyons (*c*.130 to *c*.202 AD) said that 'the glory of God is man fully alive'. God's kingdom is not built by those half-alive or half-asleep who can't be bothered, who only care about having an easy life.

Self-awareness and self-knowledge can so often remain dry, and simply a head-exercise. I have met many people who *have* insight, knowledge, and a lot of awareness, but dare not put it into practice. They stayed closed to the inner experience of the awareness 'in the gut'. All the awareness possible will not yet make a person into a 'living' person. We can listen until the cows come home, but if we do not 'hear' then we are no better off.

On the other hand, I have met the opposite too. Sally, who felt she had to keep the house spick and span, and in this way had to please her husband, and who one day said, 'I need to love myself first'. Or Danny, who had difficulties forming lasting relationships with women, who trusted a dream to open himself to an unusual relationship with a much younger woman,

Perhaps by only talking about other people I cannot convey that sense of reality and immediacy. By sharing my own experience I do not want to boast, but give one more example of how becoming alive can happen.

I had had all the intellectual knowledge for years, but never felt that I knew 'in my gut' what being committed to God was. I had not said that decisive 'yes'. On that particular day I felt compelled beyond argument to have a 'day out' and I went to the little underground chapel at Reaching Out. I sat there for about four hours. I know I sat, but for most of the time it was a real battle between God and me. I felt like Jacob, wrestling with God. In the end I said, 'You win, but now bless me'. I knew then that I had said that 'yes'. I walked home bent and unsteady like a cripple. I felt bruised and battered. But it has proved to be the experience which literally changed my life, spiritually – in that I am now able to trust God; and materially – in that soon afterwards I became a team member of Reaching Out.

Listening means coming alive. It means becoming aware and so it means responding. How and what we respond to is what life is all about. Christ, the Word, lived among us. He lived the meaning of his life, and in this way 'we saw his glory' (John 1:14). When we too are living the meaning of our lives then others will see our 'glory'. They will recognise in us the glory of God.

When we don't know our meaning and values in life, then we are drifting about, half alive, and not content with anything. 'In so far as we do not know ourselves we do not own or "appropriate" what is within us and we are that much less human' says Johnston.[8] To become aware through listening is therefore to become human. And to be human is to be the glory of God.

## References

1 Taylor, J. (1986) *A Matter of Life and Death*. London: SCM Press, p. 22.
2 Ashkenazi, L. (1986) Interview. In 'De Jerusalem', no. 38, private circulation, translated by the author.
3 World Health Organisation. Basic documents: Preamble to the constitution of the World Health Organisation.
4 Merton, T. (1968) *Zen and the Birds of Appetite*. Abbey of Gethsamani, Inc., p. 130.
5 Keirsey, D. and Bates, M. (1984) *Please Understand Me*. Del Mar, CA: Prometheus Nemesis Book Co.
6 Sacks, O. (1984) *A Leg to Stand On*. London: Pan Books, p. 108.
7 Carroll, L. (1939) *The Complete Works of Lewis Carroll*. London: The Nonesuch Press, p. 88.
8 Johnston, W. (1981) *The Mirror Mind*. London: Collins, p. 29.

# Listening to the Environment

That which surrounds us and those with whom we share
our daily lives need to be heard. Our environment is there
for our use, 'and indeed it is very good' (Gen. 1:31).

## Home

'An Englishman's home is his castle.' Has our home a
welcome mat outside, or a bridge over a moat, to be drawn
up at specific times? And are the reasons for that fear, or
selfishness, or laziness? Has this castle-home treasures in it,
and what sort of treasures? Is it all practical and stream-
lined, or are there 'useless' nooks and crannies?

Old houses sometimes have beautifully carved doors and
gateways. They have stuccoed entrances and windows.
They have room for window boxes, and they have
individually worked chimney stacks. Modern houses are
'living machines', according to the architect Le Corbusier.
Modern houses have Hoovers and mixers, freezers and
computers, and when the electricity fails, we cannot even
comfort ourselves with a cup of tea.

'Your house is your larger body' wrote Kahlil Gibran.[1]

The bricks and mortar which we call home are hugely
significant in our lives. We spend a lot of time surrounded
by them. In the business of listening to ourselves in order to
find the real meaning of our lives, we need to listen deeply
to what our houses and homes tell us about ourselves. Our
homes reflect the style of life we lead. They reflect also our

needs, our desires and our dreams. The possessions we
have in them have got there because we felt we needed or
wanted them, or someone else thought this of us and gave
us a particular item. Our homes speak about ourselves, and
reveal ourselves to those who visit us.

A tidy house does not only reveal a tidy person. It might
reveal compulsions, or an inner untidiness, or a sense of not
quite belonging here, or a futile sort of wish that someone
might arrive at any minute. We can give our home an
interpretation, but we also need to hear what it says to us:
what is its message?

Our house is our larger body: do we like it as such? Do
we respect it as such? A castle can so often also be a prison.
Olive, who is 85, has arthritis and lives alone, will often
phone up on a sunny day and say, 'You are so lucky that
you can go out'. Her world turns around her bed, distorting
the perspective on life.

In many situations escape is not actually the best
solution. Listening to ourselves cannot be done while
fleeing. We hear the word spoken to us not by running
away, but by staying put. The Desert Fathers knew this
well: 'A certain brother came to the Abbot Moses in Scete
seeking a word from him. And the old man said to him,
'Go and sit in thy cell, and thy cell shall teach thee all
things'.[2]

Our homes teach us about our relationships with
possessions and property. They teach us about roots and
how and when to recognise our own personal roots, and
how to grow them. Our homes teach us about making
choices, and about values. We choose one house rather
than another to live in; we value one kind of a house more
than another. We shape our surroundings, but long before
we learn how to do that, our surroundings have shaped us.
The houses and places where we were brought up have
contributed to our character and our values. We cannot cut
off our roots, for they will always be a part of us. But neither
can we simply take over our parents' roots and grow in
them, for that would be denying our individuality. We have
to find our own selves in and through coming in and going

out, leaving and returning (Ps. 121:8), letting go of some
things and acquiring others.

Our houses as our 'larger body' are symbols and signs of
unity and eternity. Abraham, Isaac and Jacob who 'lived in
tents . . . looked forward to a city founded, designed and
built by God' (Heb. 11:10). The 'tents' we live in now point
us towards the fulfilment of all our hopes and desires, and
the ultimate meaning of every deed and thought.


## Work

Work is often regarded as a curse and a chore. 'With sweat
on your brow shall you eat your bread' (Gen. 3:19). The
Garden of Eden was a dream; now it's a case of tilling the
soil (Gen. 3:23) for ever.

When looking at our surroundings as the things which
influence us, work must come high up on the list. I am
aware here of the role of worklessness and unemployment.
But I am not only thinking of the kind of work which is
financially rewarding and supportive, but rather of acts and
deeds in general, therefore I shall not make a special issue
of unemployment. Aliveness and responsiveness are not
characteristics only of those who work, but of all people.

Whatever work we do, it shapes us. To sit and think over
a problem, to dig the garden, to carry out a surgical
operation, to navigate a boat, to mine coal, to cook, to assist
another person in any form – any work is creative in some
way. We do it in response to a word heard or experienced.

Some of those words to mankind were 'be fruitful,
multiply, fill the earth and conquer it' (Gen. 1:28). These
words surely have more meaning than the usually accepted
one of producing descendants. Christ as the Word, the
*Logos*, saw His work in terms of bringing 'good news to the
poor, to proclaim liberty to captives and to the blind new
sight, to set the downtrodden free, and to proclaim the
Lord's year of favour' (Luke 4:18–19). In doing these tasks
we are fruitful, creative, responding to the Word.

Not all work is 'social work'. Although I have never
asked him, I have often thought that my postman has a

'vocation' for his work by the way he carries it out. Arthur is an ordained priest, and a bricklayer during the week. Gerry, a telephonist, is a deeply committed Christian. These people have 'heard' God's call to be themselves, and their work is only one expression of that, but in their 'being' they give to their work the meaning which it deserves.

It always grieves me when I hear people announced as: 'the trade unionist, John Smith' or 'the psychiatrist and lecturer, Dr Mary Jones'. We are identified by what we *do*, not by what we *are*. Work shapes us and gives us a label and an identification. But we can only *do* work – any work – because of what we *are*. When we know ourselves, then the work we do becomes less important and the *person* we are becomes important.

Most of us do many jobs, works and actions. The name of a job which we put down on a dotted line may not be what is most important at all. Many people have a nine-to-five job, and literally only come alive at 5.30 pm, when they can start with their 'real' work, be this collecting something, or studying some subject, or entertaining.

Not all work is specifically 'Christian' work, even when performed by a Christian. But all work is 'holy'. As we have been created in the image of God (Gen. 1:27), so our work of being fruitful, multiplying and filling the earth and conquering it, is doing God's work. This may give us an incentive for work, even an interpretation of it. When we listen to ourselves we also listen to the kind of work which we are creating. We need not only to *do* work, but hear it.

Hillman said in an interview: 'Psychology still tells you that tools are an extension of the hand, part of the ego, instruments of willpower. But the hand doesn't use tools, tools use the hand and teach it how to work. So to begin with, we learn about working by noticing more in detail how we actually go about working'.[3] Through work we are shaped and formed. Work is holy – and work makes us holy. '. . . to sweep a room as for thy sake makes that and the action fine'.

Much work is boring and repetitive and not stimulating. Rather than being humanised by it, people are de-

humanised by it. Even then – or particularly then – do we
need to find meaning in it. In listening to our work, our
surroundings, much so-called meaninglessness, we hear the
sounds of the earth groaning in its great act of giving birth
(Rom. 8:22) to the Word.

## Nature

We are surrounded by nature: earth, water, air and fire,
days and nights and seasons, stars, wind, heat and cold,
animate and inanimate things. Without them we would not
be maintained in life. Yet most of the time we take them all
for granted.

Frankl, in his book *Man's Search for Meaning*[4] describes
three ways by which we discover meaning in life: by doing a
deed, by experiencing a value, and by suffering. The second
of these, the experiencing of a value, happens generally
through a work of nature or culture, and also by experiencing someone. One way of discovering meaning in our life is
through nature.

Perhaps the first important point to make here is that we
do not *give* meaning to anything, but that we *discover* it. The
meaning of all things is intrinsic, but we have to learn to see
and recognise it. If we want to understand ourselves
therefore, and our place in the universe, we have to hear the
meaning of the universe, and ourselves in relation to it.

We may often ask, why are the rocks as and where they
are? And water, air and fire which wreak such havoc over
the earth, what is their meaning? But they are there, and
although people have tried to stem them and confine them,
they have not yet overwhelmed them. The charge to us is to
'fill the earth and conquer it', not to change it out of
recognition, but to wrestle with it and work with it. For that
reason we need to hear what nature has to say about itself,
and what this means for us.

What does nature say about itself? The writer of Psalm 19,
verses 1–2 states that 'the heavens declare the glory of God,
the vault of heaven proclaims his handiwork; day discourses
of it to day, night to night hands on the knowledge. No

utterance at all, no speech, no sound that anyone can hear; yet their voice goes out through all the earth, and their message to the ends of the world'. We come back again to this 'word', this message, this something which we hear. In nature, the psalmist says, this word is transmitted without sound. Nature indicates by its being itself what the message is: it is the glory of God. And man fully alive is also the glory of God. Each one of us is bidden to discover his and her own unique way of expressing this.

The sparrows have their story to tell, and so do the lilies (Matt. 6:25–34) – and so do the daisies and each pebble on the seashore, and each snowflake. None of these is forgotten or ever wasted. They teach us that this is also true of us. The glory of God is not selfish and remote, but is a participative glory. The message, the meaning in nature and all creation is: listen! Listen, and become part of this great creative act of being – being alive with each other and with God.

Frances had lost her husband when she was only 40. He had died unexpectedly, and the weeks afterwards were difficult and disorientating. About six months after the funeral she went to stay with friends in the west country. It was autumn and the nights were frosty, but the days particularly clear. One day she went for a long walk and finally climbed up a small hill. As she stood there she noticed a butterfly stretching its wings in the warm sunshine. The symbols revealed by the butterfly – of transformation, freedom, hidden and revealed parts – spoke to her forcefully. She felt able to 'let go' for the first time, and be reassured that her husband lived on.

God speaks to and through nature very powerfully: 'one word from him dried up the Sea of Reeds' (Ps. 106:9). That word permitted the people of Israel to pass from slavery to freedom, through water. Baptism, as a symbol of passing through, speaks to us of this need to be deeply immersed into nature, into all that surrounds us.

There is a very fine line between the worship of an object and the worship of the God who created the object. In some strong spiritual experience there may be no dividing line between the two. Indeed, words may not ever adequately express essentially what such an experience is. Much has been written on these aspects, and much harm has been done by dogmatism. When an experience of God through nature is real, and good, then it leads to His glory. If not, then we will have to question both the experience and our motives. However, when such an experience leads to an awareness of ourselves which commands a response, then we will have heard the true message, however badly we may put it into words.

## Media

'When a dog bites a man that is not news, but when a man bites a dog that is news', J. B. Bogart is believed to have said.

Among the things which surround us and shape us, the media surely has pride of place. The written and the spoken word is all around us. We can hardly ever escape it, even if we wanted to. Newspapers, radio and television are giving us instant access to almost anything we want to hear. Books, magazines, films and plays are ours for a small price. But there are vast quantities of information-sources which come in to us either uninvited, or because we cannot help it. Every bus has advertisements on it, and while we look for the number of the bus-route, we also see which film is in town, or which tea is the best buy.

But what has all that got to do with self-awareness and finding the meaning of our lives? We could be cynical and say that it only distracts from that goal. I don't think that it is as simple as that.

Goodman Ace said of newspapers, 'I keep reading between the lies'. Reading gives us the chance to be selective and sift what comes our way. We are shaped and influenced by what we read, and out of that our values are formed which give meaning to our lives. We have a need to trust something, and let it shape us and influence us, be this the lines of print themselves, or what is written between them.

The mass media has to do with making impressions, and the more people that can be impressed, the better. What makes impressions are usually the sad, the gory, and the sensational stories. Reading them, we can then pat our-selves on the back and say, at least I am not as bad as that, or as poor as that. It gives us a good feeling. A good story might produce the opposite effect, and make us feel miserable. We need a negative to create a positive.

We cannot escape the world in which we live, full of sounds and images. But so that we can really make a choice in what we hear we have to put these sounds and images to their opposites: to silence, and to void. In a world which is alive, silence and void are not 'nothing'; they too have their place and their meaning. If we want to make sense of the mass media, and use it for our own personal growth, and that of the whole earth, then we have always to see and hear the actual and factual, and also the mental and the spiritual, the implied. We need to listen to beyond that which is spoken, and see beyond that which is por-trayed.

### Leisure

We talk today of the leisure-industry, and we are exhorted to learn how to be at leisure, and how to use that time well. This is certainly a reversal of earlier times. Among the things which surround us, leisure has therefore more and more an important role to play.

Many of us work hard for weeks on end, working overtime and saving money, in order to have a holiday, when for two or three weeks we do absolutely nothing else except lie on a beach. We go from one extreme to another. It is almost a masochistic way of enjoying ourselves! We feel that we have to earn our holiday, otherwise it will not have been a 'real' holiday. Leisure has become another kind of 'work'.

The meaning of leisure is to be free, not to be in a hurry, and to have time at one's disposal. Leisure is an oppor-tunity to look at the world from a different angle, and perhaps in a different place. Just as the body needs sleep as part of its regular functioning, so it needs relaxation and a different pace at certain times for its continued re-creation. Not only the body, but also the mind and the soul too need this change. Leisure is not a luxury – it is a vital part of living. We need to work *and* to play.

Leisure-times are special times. Because we can be relaxed then, we are more receptive to all sorts of influences around us. It is therefore not surprising that all kinds of unusual things can happen to us, like falling in love, having spiritual experiences, becoming seriously ill, or discovering hidden talents. When we are at leisure, we find that things and events which we might ordinarily not recognise as significant, suddenly stand out, begging to be taken notice of. Holidays, like other important events, can be moments of truth.

Can we allow them their space? Are we willing to hear them speak to us? It may take some courage. That sort of listening is often an unknown kind of listening, and therefore perhaps frightening. It shows us to ourselves, but a side which we either don't know well, or would rather not know. Whenever we start listening to ourselves, we are always likely to hear unexpected things. As we start on any kind of leisure-time we should do it with an attitude of an explorer: always prepared to meet something totally unexpected.

Even in times of leisure we will meet some form of work, routine, relationships with others, old places and known settings. But now we see them as with different eyes. An ordinary house can look like a palace, and a mere stone stumbled against can be a gem. When we allow ourselves to be open and receptive, the world around is able to break in and shape us. Even the newspaper may not be full of lies any more, but pieces of news and information which we have the intellectual power to discern and analyse and enjoy. Samuel Johnson remarked once that 'all intellectual improvement arises from leisure'.

Just as we give leisure to our bodies, so we should also give leisure to our souls. Someone with a disciplined life of prayer and devotion might want to leave the prayer book at home when going on holiday, and use another form of prayer then. Or someone with no particular rule of prayer might benefit from a book of devotions used just on holidays. This may not be either frivolity or 'being good', but it may be a deep call to respond to God in an unusual way. And why? To be more open, more committed, more able to respond to the word, the message, in the ways it wants to reveal itself to us.

This can often happen on holiday. But equally it may happen by reading a book, seeing a film, sharing a meal with someone, visiting an exhibition. When we are aware of the moment, then we are aware of what it might say to us. We enable ourselves to listen. Listening to ourselves is a far-reaching activity. It leads us to heights and depths which we might never guess. It leads us into ecstasies and into deep suffering with others and with God. Leisure may only be one trigger for any of these states. When something does call us, or move us while relaxed, it is perhaps especially unexpected, or moving, but it is always real. It may shake us, and it will certainly contribute to 'make' us.

## Life Events

Whenever there is an occasion to look back over our lives, it is not the ordinary days which stand out, but the extraordinary ones. By these I mean both the joyful and the sorrowful days. Life's great events shape us and mark us. To what extent do we let them do this?

Some of these life events can be planned, like marriage and great celebrations of anniversaries and parties for various reasons. But many events cannot be planned nor even foreseen. Accidents, illnesses and death come upon us unbidden and often catch us unawares, sleeping. They wake us up and make us painfully aware of ourselves. I would like first to look at the unplanned events in our lives.

The goal of becoming aware through listening is to find

meaning in life. And meaning, as Frankl points out, comes to us – is discovered by us – through the values which we hold. Some of these values come alive to us by the ways in which we react to unfortunate circumstances over which we have no control, such as our own and other people's suffering. The way in which we respond to such events shows us and others what sort of people we are.

Because such events are unplanned and uncalled-for we cannot truly prepare for them. They will never come in the way we expected them, or when we expected them. By being aware of ourselves and life around us – by being awake – we are, however, more in a position to face such events. We can handle them, rather than be swamped by them; we can 'look them in the eye' straight away, and don't first have to rub the sleep out of our own eyes.

But it is not a staying awake in case something bad or sad might happen. That would not be aliveness, but fear. The meaning towards which we work is not something future, but always something present, now, immediate. A big event is something 'now', and that is why such big events give our lives particular meaning. We can really only prepare for big events by taking small events seriously. The many small unfortunate circumstances which we meet with every day shape the direction and meaning of our lives. Are we willing to pay attention to them today? Peter, a middle-aged man, wrote after the death of his father, 'the turmoil is well below the surface and is now absorbed into my own wondering of what I really ought to be doing'. Not only a death, but any kind of loss – illness, loss of job, divorce, or the children moving away – is a turning point. It depends on us what sort of a turning point we make of it.

The paradox with many events is that what for one person may be a loss is for another a gain. A marriage is a 'giving away' for the parents, and a great start for the couple concerned. Whichever side we are on at a wedding, we are present at a ceremony of changing relationships, and sanctifying the change. Without such rituals the gains and losses are not made 'legitimate' and therefore they are often not handled well.

Down the ages people have marked the great events in their lives with some ritual or ceremony. For many of us these rites of passage have nowadays lost significance. We still celebrate birth, marriage and death, but many other events get overlooked. Coming of age often means simply a bigger party than usual, but with none of the attendant ceremonies of passing from childhood to adulthood.

The other event – the coming of old age – is generally only celebrated with a party when leaving work. Rather than celebrating wisdom and the acquisition of a privileged position in the family, it is often seen as a passage from useful to useless life. No wonder that people are marked so profoundly by it. When we are not used to celebrate many significant events in our lives, one such as retirement can be devastating.

We *do* celebrate events like moving house, and special anniversaries, promotion, or new relationships. But as well as the outer event we need to celebrate the inner event. Great joys and great sorrows mark us. The gospels tell us of people celebrating the finding of a lost sheep and lost coin (Luke 15:4–10), and even a lost son (Luke 15:11–32). These were events which had marked the people concerned, and to make their feelings legitimate, they had a celebration. If we don't mark them, then they don't mark us – we walk by them half asleep, not bothering.

When we are aware and awake then we are also able to discern which events need to mark us. We allow ourselves to be marked, and in this way we respond to the event. We hear what it has to say to us. We sit down with it. When we allow the big events truly to come into our lives, then they will not shock us or dismay us. We recognise them as necessary parts of life. When we listen to their meaning, then they will direct us to the meaning of all life, and ours in particular.

## World Events

It is not only our own events which shape us, but other people's events and sufferings too. Self-awareness does

not only come from and through the immediate surroundings, but from all that does go on and has gone on around
us.

Hardly a day goes by that we do not hear of some
disaster somewhere. Floods, famine, plane crashes, abduc-
tions, killings and bombs are only among the most widely
publicised. With so much of it around we almost have to
become dulled to the pain of it. In what way then do we
listen to these events which come in to us unbidden? Do we
shut them up, or shut ourselves up? Or do we listen and
hear? The world is becoming smaller and smaller, and what
happens around the globe is immediately available to us.
By not buying the newspaper and not watching the
television, we may not know what is going on around us. By
reading the newspaper and then forgetting what we have
read we close ourselves off. By sending a cheque to the
worthiest cause we make ourselves feel good. In this way we
escape an involvement. A real and true response is always
active and involving. Do we need to get up from our sleep
and actually go somewhere, do something? What *is* our
response to what we hear such events say to us?

It is not only the events now which shape us. Events in
history affect us and shape us. Movements of people,
migrations, wars and disasters from the past are our
inheritance. Our faith affirms that we 'have been buried
with Christ' (Col. 2:12). We believe this in faith, and yet it
is also a fact of history which we take part in.

Not many other happenings in history claim such a
worldwide and spiritual significance. The fact of being
human makes us involved in the world around us. As we
listen to such events, and what they say to us; as we become
aware of ourselves in history, we might ask, how are we
now shaping the lives of those who come after us? This is
not only an intellectual exercise, but also a practical, an
emotional and a spiritual one. Awareness must lead to
some response and commitment. On our awareness and
our response now depends the future.

In 1987 there were several disasters in Britain which
touched people deeply: the sinking of the ferry at Zeebrugge,

the Hungerford shootings, and the King's Cross fire. In what way were you touched by those events? What did they say to you then? What do they still say to you now? Perhaps you might like to make a note, or start a diary and write down some of the thoughts which come to you while reading these pages. All thoughts which jolt us in any way are meaningful and helpful. Sometimes to go back to a particular one – when it was recorded – can be revealing later even if at the time it was no more than noted down. If words are not particularly helpful to you, you might make a drawing or painting, or record in symbolic language where awareness is leading you while you are using this book.

In December 1987 the signing of the nuclear arms reduction treaty took place. This event happened in Advent, when we traditionally look at 'the last things': death, judgement, heaven, hell. I found it personally significant that this treaty to reduce the threat of war took place in Advent. Global and man-made death and hell seem to have been reduced. An event in history had its spiritual counterpart. Material and spiritual things came together. This gives me hope that the material and spiritual are perhaps not as far apart as many people claim. This event spoke to me of hope. It will have spoken of other things to other people. It may not be the details of what such events say which matter, but that we have listened to them and to us, and heard what each has to say to the other.

## Routine and Ordinary Things

We are marked by the highlights of special events. But we are equally marked by much routine. Washing, cleaning, shopping, travelling to and from work, the rituals of getting up and going to bed, paying bills, watering the plants, and so many things – we do them almost blindfold and without giving too much thought to them. Indeed, if we did give them thought they might almost become unbearable. We would begin to do them awkwardly and they might take far

more time then. They have become routine to save us time
and energy.

The fact that we do so much by routine and without
thinking might be very significant. We have many more
humdrum things in our lives than special things. What does
that say about us, and to us? Are we so busy that we don't
have time for special times and special things? Are we so
busy that we cannot give enough attention to the ordinary
and the commonplace? And what are we so busy with? The
daily little events in our lives are all there to be part of the
pattern of life in general, and we need to hear them speak to
us as much as the big events.

No tube journey is the same. No shopping trip quite like
the one before. No day is the same, therefore no shower or
shave is quite the same. Each routine thing has its own
highlight and silver lining. We should learn not to walk by
but to treasure these things because they are there in our
path and as such are there to shape that path, and guide us
towards our goal

'Try to discover what the Lord wants of you . . . wake up
from your sleep . . . be very careful . . . do not be
thoughtless . . .' (Eph. 5:10–17). These are not only
instructions for spiritual growth, but for personal living
too. The physical and spiritual are dependent on each
other, and one grows through and because of the other.
We live lives acceptable to God when we also recognise
Him in the everyday and common-or-garden things and
events.

But there are also other small and so-called uneventful
things in our lives. These are not routine, but so insignifi-
cant that we could easily overlook them. Yet they bring
light and colour into a day.

A letter from someone you thought about a few days ago
arrives today. You walk past a garden and today you smell
a rose which you had not noticed before. A spider web
glistens with the dew. A child gives you a smile. Thousands
– millions – of such events make life full and exciting. But
we need to have eyes to see (Mark 8:18) and minds which

are open to receive the messages to us of these little ordinary miracles.

And there are not only the silent and inanimate events which turn an ordinary moment into a special one. The innumerable comments and remarks, spoken and written, which we are aware of all around us, are no less wonderfull. Jokes are a tonic. But so are the many unwanted and unprepared quips. My favourites were both spoken by children: 'Mummy, how can we make mud?' and a little boy in hospital who had to give a specimen of his water: 'It's difficult to do the toilet in a kettle'.

The unexpected, the overheard, the unprepared – these are the little things in life. But how often have the little things been preferred to the big and the mighty? The Kingdom of God belongs to little children (Mark 10:14). The last will be the first (Matt. 19:30). Small is beautiful.

The routine, ordinary things in life have their place as routine. They help us to get through the day without too much effort. But every now and again they reverse roles with the important things. At such times we should be noticing what is happening. We should be prepared to accept what is happening. When we are able to hear the message or music of these events, then are we awake and capable of giving a response. In some of them we will meet the living God.

### Art

In the collection of things which surround and influence us the audio-visual arts are never far away. We need not only think of pictures in galleries and concerts in halls. Every tune which comes from a radio, and every card pinned to a wall is artistic. Each in their turn and in their place says something to us, and reveals something about us.

These two forms of art are predominantly received through seeing and hearing. Some art is to be touched, and even smelt, but mostly it is seen and heard. Rabbi Ashkenazi[5] makes an interesting point about seeing and hearing. 'Listening comes first, and only those who have known how to listen in truth will be called to seeing'. God did not reveal himself to his people in any form, but as the 'Word'. He did not reveal himself with a proper name, but as a statement: Yahweh – I am who I am. Only those who have learnt how to listen to the spoken word can then go on to see it when it is written down in a book.

But what has this to do with art? I believe that the art which we have around us has to speak to us very deeply first of all. When we know how to hear it, then can we also appreciate it by seeing its message. Gibran says, 'beauty is eternity gazing at itself in a mirror. But you are eternity and you are the mirror'.[6] The message of any beauty is that it reflects ourselves, and it reflects also the image and likeness of God (Gen. 1:27). Before we can 'see' that, we have to 'hear' it. That is why we hear ourselves.

We are surrounded by art and beauty. This may be one reason why we have become so deaf to much of what we actually hear. We find it difficult to be so absorbed in a piece of music that we hear it speak its message. Music may stimulate us, make us joyful, relax us, lull us to sleep. It should heal, guide, inspire and take us out of ourselves. I remember one day in Jerusalem, in the church of St Anne, a group of American pilgrims sang 'Amazing Grace', and the whole building sang. I could not help but to join in singing as loud as I could, while tears rolled down my cheeks. The words, the sound and the building all combined to make this an experience of 'eternity' for me.

A work of art need not be a well recognised masterpiece before it can speak a message to us. The scribbles of a small child and the tune extracted out of a harmonica can speak just as powerfully as any symphony or the Mona Lisa. What matters is not the picture or tune itself, but what they convey. What matters is that we hear within us the call to be more like the image of God created within us. It is a call to be more Christ-like.

## Worship

For us Christians, worship must surely be one of those

activities which shape and influence us profoundly. Prayer and worship are those activities which are inborn and instinctual to anyone who calls God Father.

I shall look at private prayer in the next chapter. Here the emphasis is on formal worship, on services in a church, or a gathering of people for the purpose of divine worship. Church services are not always terribly inspiring. The buildings are often drab and too big, the hymns too ancient and little relevant to today, and the sermon, well . . . But divine worship is not just here to inspire us. It is here for us to worship God and to tell each other of His love and glory and power. Yet the worship itself influences us, and the kind of worship which we take part in also says of us who we are.

So far, in this 'litany' of the environment which I have detailed as marking and forming us, worship comes not only at the end, but also at the beginning and in the middle, and at every point in between.

Once we start being aware of ourselves and our surroundings, we become aware of the holiness of all things. Once we look on any object as having intrinsic worth and by listening to it, we hear in it and through it that eternal word. What the message of that word is will vary from time to time, and from person to person. Essentially it has always to do with love. But now one aspect becomes more important, now another. When we are awake and aware, we will, however, hear the word which is addressed to us *now* and *here*. So it is also with worship. The dullest, most uninteresting service has its word, its message to convey, and we are indeed happy if we hear that message. A truly inspiring service may of course speak even more powerfully.

Every aspect of every service of worship is important in itself. When we see it as such, then every act of worship is creative. In its praise of God it is also creating us, the worshippers, the people, in that it contributes to our ability to respond to that praise. It liberates us, gives us peace, and above all gives us a sense of meaning in our lives.

Some services are rich in symbols and artistry, and some are devoid of any external stimuli. Some of the Norman churches and cathedrals are stark and plain, and in their very simplicity ask the worshippers to lift their hearts to God and Him alone. Other churches are full of baroque angels and cherubs. They too speak of God, but differently.

One of the joys of the ecumenical movement is that we can be more free and more 'at home' in each other's churches and learn from each other different ways of worship. Ecumenism does not ask us necessarily to change, but to be open to what we might hear.

In Chapter 1 I highlighted the different temperaments. Each temperament is also suited to a different type of worship and spirituality. Some forms of worhsip and spirituality put much emphasis on creative imagination and use Bible passages to apply to today's situations. Other people prefer to remember the actual events in salvation history. The services of Holy Week and Easter as they are celebrated in the catholic traditions are a good example of this. Yet another type of person will prefer reflective meditation and strive to attain virtue. A fourth type of person will be happiest when actually taking part in celebrations which are spontaneous, and perhaps impulsive. Their prayer is short, sharp, and to the point. Ideally, any worship would incorporate all these types of spirituality, so that everybody gets fulfilment of their various needs. Rather than condemn or dismiss some types of worship, we should listen and hear what they have to say to us and how through them we become more whole and more holy.

Divine services are very much like life: they are an alternation of giving and receiving. Sunday by Sunday we are refreshed and renewed. We are assured of God's love and grace. But for that to happen we bring ourselves to the place of refreshment. We may come in our Sunday best, but really we come, just as we are.

I for one am pleased that the Anglican church has dropped the confession which started Matins and Evensong not with assurances of God's presence, but with us being miserable offenders who have no health in us. These things are true, but only in relation to other factors. Worship itself has the capacity to make us aware of ourselves as we truly are. We are led to take our stand before God with thanksgiving and confession. We do not receive more grace when we have grovelled more. We *are* God's servants, but we are also His friends (John 15:13) and His likeness. When we are able to hear the word of the worship – then we are also able to respond with the word of love. That must be the meaning of all listening and hearing, and searching.

## Relationships

People and relationships are the joys of life, and they often also cause the pains of life. Joys and sorrows usually have one and the same source.

So far we have looked mainly at 'things' which surround and influence us. The people who surround us shape us just as much, if not more. I want to look here at the kinds of relationships we have with people in general, not at particular people.

Relationships come in many forms and guises. There are relationships between parents and children, friends and friends, employer and employee, tradesman and buyer, doctor and patient, husband and wife, performers and audience, lawyers and prisoners. There are the relationships between people together in a crowded train, on a course, on a holiday beach, or in a hospital ward. They don't know each other, but they share a common aim for a particular time. We don't know each other, but should the going get rough, we would probably band together to defend our cause.

Then there are the numerous degrees of friendship, ranging from acquaintance, via companions, fellows, mates and pals to associates and bosom friends. The degree of importance of these varies with the need we share with each of the people concerned.

Some of the people who surround us measure their popularity by the number of Christmas cards they get, others by how many pub landlords know their name. Some people are known more than they know. Some have a capacity to make friends with everyone they meet; others remain aloof or alone. Some people's faces are remembered; others will go totally unnoticed. These people share life with us, and we with them. They make us aware of our strong points and our inadequacies. As we listen to what they say to us in their stories and conversations, so we listen with an inner ear to what they do *not* say with words, but imply. The impressions they make on us, the influences we allow them to have on us, and we have on them – these are the kind of things which we need to listen to and hear.

Each relationship which we have is different, and says different things to us and about us. We need to listen to the various connections and affinities which we have. In order to grow and to learn we need to rub shoulders with all sorts of people. In so doing we need to view the world not only from our standpoint, but also from the other's in a relationship. We need to hear what the other is about, and what the relationship says about us.

Olive was very ill in hospital. She knew she had not much time left. She asked the librarian to leave her a copy of *Winnie the Pooh*. When her two sisters visited she recognised them, but was unable to speak to them. They were distressed at her condition and spoke to one of the nurses. The nurse told them that Olive might die quite soon, but that she could probably still hear what they were saying. *Winnie the Pooh* lay open on the bed at the page which Olive had reached before getting too weak to hold the book. The sisters were devout Christians and one of them took a prayer book out. Somehow, this stayed closed, but they took it in turns to read aloud from *Winnie the Pooh*. Only when they had finished reading did they realise that Olive had quietly died in the meantime.

It has been said that before we dare to challenge others and their ways of being and doing, we need to be able to challenge ourselves, and our ways of being and doing. This can never be done in the abstract, but only ever in relation to people, to those who shape our lives with us. When we listen to people and their relationships with us we are unlikely to hear any talk of right and wrong; relationships are not that simple. But we probably hear of ways and means of making the relationship better and of deepening its spirit. Just as relationships are not exclusive, so they are not to be used and exploited. They are to be advanced and to be cared for.

Sometimes, we say, we have done everything to make a particular relationship better, but nothing works. A friendship or an acquaintance can be broken off, but relationships within families are not so easy. We cannot usually break away from family ties without much heartache. When a relationship does break down, we need to be aware of two things: (a) that for this to happen it takes both partners in that relationship, and (b) that we can only truly bear our own part, and not that of the other person as well. Much pain is caused by people not knowing what is their own luggage and what is the other person's luggage. Either shrugging off our legitimate responsibility, or taking upon ourselves the pain of others is not usually helpful. When we see clearly what needs to be done in a particular situation, then we will probably have listened to ourselves, to the other person, and to the relationship and heard which is the part each has to play.

Because relationships are so difficult, they teach us so very much. There is a constant listening and responding movement going on between two people. And what goes on between people is mirrored in what goes on between a person and God. We do not create meaning in life, but we discover it, and we discover it supremely in and through the various relationships which we have. The relationships change, and our needs change, but through them all emerges the meaning, the goal, of each person's life. That goal is not obvious from the start, but has to be searched for. 'Search, and you will find' (Matt. 7:7). Search the secrets of people and of relationships, and you will find yourself.

## References

1 Gibran, K. (1926) *The Prophet*. London: W.Heinemann Ltd (1980 edition), p. 83.

2 Waddell, H. (1962) *The Desert Fathers*. London: Collins, p. 83.
3 Hillman, J. (1988) The soul at work. Resurgence, Issue 128, pp. 4–7.
4 Frankl, V. E. (1962) *Man's Search for Meaning*. London: Hodder & Stoughton, p. 113.
5 Ashkenazi, L. (1986) Interview. In 'De Jerusalem'. no. 38. Private circulation. Translated by the author.
6 Gibran, K. *op cit*. p. 89.

3

# Listening to and with the Soul

I am using the word 'soul' for all aspects of the inner being: mind, spirit, inner voice, self; leaving it to the reader to hear which word or concept is most appropriate for her or him.

## Listening to the Soul

Our bodies and surroundings find their echo within ourselves, in the soul. Or rather, the soul echoes what happens outside. Inner and outer are in harmony, or when one is not well tuned, then the other does not play well.

The soul is not something which we can locate and feel, like the body. Yet we are aware of an inner life which is more than thoughts and feelings. The soul is that which gives us life, makes us real, and at times wakes us up. But we are able to listen to it or shut it up, take it seriously or ignore it.

Listening to the soul is not necessarily more difficult than listening to the body and the surroundings. But it is different. In the soul we can hide things which we cannot hide in the body. And we do hide – and have hidden – a great many things inside. As we listen to the soul we become aware of great stores of 'things both new and old' (Matt. 13:52). To examine these stores usually takes a long time. This can be difficult, but it is always deeply liberating and affirming.

What are the ways in which the soul speaks to us? Prayer

is perhaps the best-known way of listening to the soul. Sometimes it is in speaking a prayer that we hear ourselves say something which we cannot quite account for. Sometimes it is in being silent that a word or a sentence comes alive for that moment.

Philippa had become aware that she was helping people who came to her more effectively recently. It was the day before Whitsun, and she thought that she did not quite understand what the Holy Spirit meant in her life. So she prayed that she might come to a deeper insight and awareness of the Spirit. During the sermon on Whit Sunday at the service she attended, the preacher spoke about the power of the Spirit. Then she knew that that was what she had actually experienced through her work but had not been able to put into words or connect with the Spirit. She remembered 'St Patrick's Breast-plate': 'I bind unto myself today, the strong name of the Trinity'.

Sometimes we become aware of the soul through dreams, or in a conversation, during worship or when visiting special places. Ray's wife had died a few months earlier. She had been a devout Roman Catholic, and some time before her death she had gone on a pilgramage to Lourdes where she had found great strength. Ray wasn't quite convinced by such practices but felt a need to test his faith. His two sons encouraged him to go to Lourdes as a helper, and he thought that that was a good idea. A few days after his return he summed up his experience saying, 'Now I know that my Redeemer lives'.

Ray had felt a stirring in his soul but did not quite know what it was about. His sons helped to put that 'stirring' on a particular path, and this enabled Ray to hear what he needed to hear. When one of his sons died tragically a few weeks later he was able to cope remarkably well.

When counselling a person I often come to a point where I feel stuck or inadequate. Realising this, but believing that God is at work in both of us, I often make a silent prayer, 'Help! Over to you', and trusting in that, an opening usually seems right in front of me. Accepting my helplessness and acknowledging God's help often releases the free flow of grace.

These are only some of the ways in which we listen to that inner life. Temperament and particular circumstances will give us different opportunities and forms of expressions and experiences. As long as these are right for us, they are right in themselves.

Listening to the soul brings the outer and inner lives together. There are many people living their lives totally on the outer level. They centre their lives on their job, possessions, maybe a partner. Society in general puts a lot of emphasis on getting on and being self-reliant. Listening to the soul means occasionally having to stand still and stand apart, perhaps saying 'No', or 'Enough'. Having never been encouraged in these things, people don't know where to start. So they think that going through life like a whirlwind 'doing good', is a virtue. A change of circumstances can literally make their world fall apart.

Dan had been a successful writer and journalist, turning out books and articles with admirable speed and always keeping his deadlines. He was also very busy in his local church, sitting on committees and generally seeing that 'things are done'. He kept this up long beyond retirement age. A severe car accident immobilised him for a time, but he got over it and thought he would carry on, for after all, he was not dependent on anyone else. But the accident left him more severely handicapped than he had bargained for and he had to rely on unknown neighbours, home helps and nurses. He couldn't understand why his neighbours preferred to stay in bed rather than bring him his breakfast; he was rude to the nurses who washed him, and his home help seldom got a 'please' or 'thank you'. He had not heard within himself that other things than success and order also mattered.

Listening to the soul is about finding an inner freedom and peace which are able to go beyond the often harsh realities of outer life. But they are not always what we expect them to be. Peace is not a desert island, but a wholeness which has come out of much listening, wrestling, and not being afraid of meeting some skeletons in the hidden cupboards of the soul.

Most of all, as we listen to the soul, we listen to God. Many people feel that God is the great judge, and once we listen to Him we will hear of things which we should have done and haven't, or have done and shouldn't. They cannot quite square this with their need to feel loved. The truth is that if we are looking for a judge we will always find one: our own conscience condemns us. But when we are looking for love in the soul we will find that too: in God who is only mercy and compassion.

## Listening with the Soul

The soul has a great capacity to listen and as a result is full of hidden stores. The soul has heard from the beginning things which speak of love, of tender care, and of calling God Father, *Abba*. The soul is in conversation with God, listening and speaking, hearing the word and responding to it simply by saying Father.

The Hebrew word *Abba* resembles the first sounds which a child makes, 'ab – ba'. Similarly with mother: *Eema*. Buddhists practice the word 'OM' as an expression of faith. Perhaps stop here for a moment, and try to make a very simple sound and offer it as your response to God. Stay with the sound for as long as it has meaning for you. Henry Nouwen calls that listening with the soul the 'creative contact with the ground of our own life'.[1]

As we listen to the soul we become aware that God is not 'out there', but He is within. The soul is 'god-shaped', and the more we listen to the soul, the more we become like God. What sorts of things do we hear when we listen with the soul? Listening with the soul will always be a challenge.

Helen was making a retreat, and meditated on the words from scriptures, 'I am standing at the door, knocking. If one of you hears me calling and opens the door, I will come in and share his meal' (Rev. 3:20) and 'I am the gate' (John 10:9) and 'I, the light, have come into the world'

(John 12:46). As she listened deeply within herself she became aware that she had no food to share with anybody. She felt spiritually poor and starving. She felt hemmed in and unable to escape because Christ was everywhere and He even was the door! She was not pleased that He was the light, because she was too much aware of her own darkness. She stayed with these images – she couldn't escape them – although they were very painful and made her angry. On the last morning of her retreat another image came: Christ *calling* her through the door of her own heart and soul.

God will always challenge us to become more like Him, be more willing instruments, and more loving to ourselves and others. The challenge is not always the same, and not always to be on the move. As we listen to God we hear of destroying and of building; of mourning and dancing; of keeping and throwing away; of keeping silent and speaking (Eccles. 3:2–8); of going back to where we have come from (1 Kings 19:15), or going where we would rather not go (John 21:18). When we have truly listened we know that we cannot make any other response than the one which we are asked to make. This is the hallmark of that kind of listening. A response to true listening is never in our own interest *only*, but always to the glory of God and those around us.

### Needs

Listening to our surroundings makes us receptive to listen to the things within. But the outside and the inside are not two different things, they are two aspects of the same whole. One of the first things which we meet when we 'look inwards' are our needs. We often confuse needs with wants, and I would like to highlight both. Needs are basic to living; wants are the icing on it.

Maslow in his now famous 'Hierarchy of Needs'[2] details five levels of needs as the primary influence on our behaviour. He goes on to say that we can understand ourselves best by developing an awareness of those needs which are unsatisfied. At the bottom of this hierarchy are the basic physiological needs, such as hunger and thirst.

Then follow the safety needs: we need to feel secure and out of danger. At the third level are the needs of belongingness and love, to be accepted and to affiliate with others. Higher up are our needs for esteem, achieving, gaining approval, and being competent. At the top are the needs for self-actualisation: we need to find self-fulfilment and realise our own potential. When the lower needs are not met then we are not in a position to meet the higher needs. Conversely, if there is no satisfaction of the higher needs, then an individual may return to a state of fulfilling only the needs at a lower level. To find our true direction in life we have to attend to all the different needs.

To put these concepts into the language of this book, we have a need to listen and a need to be heard. The basic commandment to us is to listen: 'Listen, Israel, the Lord our God is the one Lord' (Mark 12:29). This is today still the first and last prayer of every Jew. Listen – hear. If we want to understand our needs we need to listen to our-selves. If we want to understand others, we needs to listen to them. If we want to understand God we need to listen to Him, and to hear that He is one. Out of His unity comes the unity of all humanity, and all things.

The four temperaments have quite distinctive needs. In listening to ourselves we become aware that we have needs which others may not recognise. I will highlight simply *some* of these needs as examples.

Introverted people, as I have said already, need to be alone often. They need time to 'just be' and need frequent changes and holidays. Extroverted people need to be in company with other people, talking, playing and working with others. Intuitive people need to be able to speculate, see a future ahead of themselves, and make use in particular of imagingation, intuition, and hunches. On the other hand, sensate people need facts; they need realities, experiences and be able to make decisions.

A thinking person needs to work with principles, logic, criteria, arguments and analyses. He (more often than she) prefers to make a choice on an impersonal basis. A feeling person is the opposite, and needs to be aware of emotions and devotions, and is at home with anything personal. The judging person needs to have things in order, work to deadlines and be well planned. A perceiving person can only function well when there is flexibility, play, and process rather than goals.

These are real needs for each person in order to develop. Difficulties arise when people do not recognise another's needs. Sensate persons, for instance, will likely get irritated with thinking persons because their needs are different. No wonder that there is so much misunderstanding between people! The sources of many relationship problems lie here. When we listen to the other's needs we will be less frustrated and more accepting of each other's different needs, and at the same time help that other person.

Some of these needs are practical, some are needs of the soul. The introverted person's need to be alone is a practical need, but it is also a need of the soul because the soul 'functions' best according to its need in silence. When we recognise our needs as whole persons, we gradually begin to know which is the one need we have (Luke 10:42) and pursue that.

To know our particular needs gives us the possibility to recognise when and where they are not met. We need not only to listen, but we also need to be heard.

## Wants, Wishes and Desires

'The One Who Has The Most Toys When They Die, Wins!'. So, apparently, goes the inscription on an old American licence-plate.

In our day and age, every kind of advertisement makes us believe that we don't only want something, but that we actually need it. When we therefore look at our needs, we have to be careful to distinguish between actual needs and actual wants. When we look into ourselves and listen to what is there, we will probably find many wishes. Some will be very good and legitimate, and some will be the sorts of wishes which replace real wakefulness. We wish that something would happen. We would like life to be different.

We think that the pain should go away. We want health, and rail against the body when we haven't got it. We want happiness, and blame the family when it doesn't come. We want success, and criticise the company or the government when we cannot have it. We want an easy life, and cry out against God when we get the opposite.

The difficulty is that we need all these things for our growth and fulfilment as persons. We know our needs – but we want them on our terms. This is the sticking point. Yet we are asked to care about the essentials first – the Kingdom of God's righteousness – and then we will know how to deal also with the less urgent needs (Matt. 6:31–34).

Wants and wishes are not superfluous, nor are they somehow wrong. They are often the first intimations that something is not as it should be. We need therefore to listen to these wishes. And when we do listen to them, then we will be able to know them for what they are.

Jean, a qualified nurse, expressed a great desire to train as a policewoman with the Metropolitan Police. After talking with a friend about it she realised that this would simply be going from one secure hierarchy to another, but that being in the Met held more prestige in the eyes of her family. She decided against the move, and instead to look at the issues of prestige and acceptability in her family, and of security in herself.

There is a difference between wants and hopes. We wish someone well, but that does not depend on us, except to the degree that we are willing to work for the wellbeing of another, be this by direct involvement or by prayerful intercession. A wish will remain an empty concept unless we do something about it.

To want peace and harmony is perhaps even more elusive. Who does not want peace? But just saying it will not bring it about. That sort of wish *can* be a cop-out: we know full well that we are impotent as ordinary individuals to do anything about world peace. To say that we want it just makes us feel better and we imagine that others will admire us for saying it. But unless we actually show that we do something, we are simply 'a gong booming or a cymbal clashing' (1 Cor. 13:1).

What we hear when we listen to what is inside of ourselves is often contradictory and painful. It shows us in our true colours. We should be grateful for that insight, because it makes us grow and become that for which we were created.

## The Shadow

It was C. G. Jung[3] who coined the term 'the shadow' for that part of the personality which is unconscious, unpleasant and insufficiently developed. Yet the shadow is not the whole of the unconscious personality. It also points to factors which come at a person from outside, and indeed it has aspects of the personality which might just as well be conscious.

Jung points out that the unconscious can make itself felt either in a helpful or a negative form. It is important to understand that the shadow shows us the positive side of ourselves as well as the negative. It shows us particularly the insufficiently developed functions. For many people – I would say most of the ones I meet – it is much harder to believe in the essential goodness of themselves than in the negative and destructive aspects. The shadow helps us to understand both parts of ourselves better.

When we give ourselves permission to listen to ourselves, then the shadow can come alive. It is always there, but we don't always acknowledge it. Like the physical shadow, we see the personality-shadow only when there is some bright light shining on us. A great insight, a dream, a relaxed and receptive mood, or a truth spoken about us by a friend may all be such lights. Such instances often make us first angry, then perplexed and sometimes speechless (what *can* we say?). After that begins a time of self-awareness and adjustment which may last a very long time and sometimes be painful. Some re-arrangement in the store of the soul is taking place.

During the retreat which Helen was making (pp. 46–7)

she had become aware of being hemmed in and in darkness
inside her. The text from scripture she was given to
meditate on was 'Do you want to be well again?' (John 5:6).
She could not answer, but was aware that like the man to
whom Jesus had addressed the question, she had been 'sick'
with resentments, regrets and resistances for very many
years. These had concerned in particular her mother and
other authority figures.

It is no wonder that many people would rather not have
anything to do with the shadow sides of themselves. They
recognise that these are the murky depths and instinctively
they turn away because they know that they face the
psychological equivalent of the labours of Hercules. This
Greek hero performed twelve immense tasks, the first of
which was to clean up the Aegean stables. In one day he
had to get rid of the dung of hundreds of horses from many
decades. Years of accumulated filth have to be cleared
away and cleansed and purified. From long acquaintance
with ourselves we know that the struggle to integrate the
forces of the unconscious and untamed parts of ourselves
with the conscious is demanding, and often not possible
alone.

Like the Greeks, the Bible uses images to describe such
forces. Elijah was driven into the desert to hide in the Wadi
Cherith and there be fed by ravens (1 Kings 17:2–6). King
Nebuchadnezzar's heart 'grew completely animal; he lived
with the wild asses; he fed on grass like the oxen; his body
was drenched by the dew of heaven' (Dan. 5:21). The
psalmist is aware of a herd of bulls surrounding him (Ps.
22:12) and a pack of dogs (v. 16). Christ was in the wilderness with the wild beasts (Mark 1:13). It is significant that
as Christ became aware of Himself, and of these wild and
lower aspects of Himself, He did not banish them. He
stayed with them for forty days. He truly listened to His
soul. When He had heard all that He needed to hear from
them, then was He ready for the 'higher' things – for the
angels, who came and served Him (v. 13).

It was only when Helen had recognised her dark,
shadowy side, and acknowledged it, that she was able to cry

and in this way feel forgiveness surge through her. It took her some time even afterwards to feel the impact of this. She needed to change her attitude particularly to her mother, and this was far from easy.

In Jung's terms the shadow also represents *Anima*, the feminine principle, and *Animus*, the masculine principle, within. They are mainly understood in terms of *anima* forces in the man and *animus* forces in the woman. But the *anima* also represents deep and therefore untapped sources of femininity in the woman, and *animus* in the man. It is not a question of becoming more male or female to understand ourselves better, but it is a question of integrating the two aspects of our nature, making them whole. This will give us the possibility and the necessary strength and belief to trust this quest of the shadow, and not be afraid of what we find. It gives us also the strength and belief that the *anima* in man and the *animus* in the woman are here to help us to become more complete beings by leading us to that goal and meaning of life.

*Anima* and *animus* are like shorthand terms for the two main archetypes of the personality. Of necessity there are many other such archetypes which we meet in our shadow. These have been described as 'first principles which govern the forces and patterns of life, (and) forces simultaneously at work in nature and in man'.[4]

The symbolic figures of father, brother, husband and son all belong to the woman's psyche. Other male figures, such as black knights and princes, priests, satyrs and giants all have their place in the development of the personality. They point us to aspects of ourselves which we might have neglected or which need attention at the moment.

Similarly for men, the symbolic figures are mother, sister, wife and daughter first of all. But other relevant symbols are nymphs, graces, white goddesses and witches. Signs like the moon represent the *anima* as do birds and white harts. Recognising such symbols as parts of our own and the collective unconscious will give us the power to unlock riddles, making them into working tools for growth.

There are many aspects to the shadow, *anima* and *animus*,

and any of the archetypes which could be used as examples.
I would like to take just one to illustrate these concepts a
little.

Johnson[5] relates a Chinese parable: 'A man stands on the
mountain top at dawn and holds forth his hands, palms up,
to say the creative yes. A woman stands on the mountain
top at dawn and holds forth her hands, palms down, to say
the creative no'. I find this parable significant for several
reasons. Firstly, both the man and the woman are together.
Male and female belong together, not only in gender terms,
but throughout nature there always are both the separate
and the together aspects of each being. The two figures are
on the mountain top. God has often revealed Himself on
mountains. God met Moses on the mountain (Exod. 19).
The transfiguration of Christ took place on a mountain
(Luke 8:28–36), and indeed the crucifixion was on a
mountain (Luke 23:33). On the mountain we become truly
what we are.

Like the Chinese parable, the revelation of God to His
people Israel took place in the morning (Exod. 19:16). The
morning is the time of meeting with God. On waking, we
gaze to fill ourselves with His likeness (Ps. 17:15). Indeed,
'each morning he wakes me to hear, to listen like a disciple'
(Isa. 50:4). Each day is new, and a new challenge to listen,
with the body and the soul, and thus to find God. 'This is
the day made memorable by the Lord, what immense joy
for us' (Ps. 118:24).

While Helen was particularly listening to and with her
soul during her retreat, she woke up several mornings with
new insights and new images for her meditation. This was
particularly striking on the last day. Like a reward for her
effort she was given an image which led her back into her
working life but with a new vision and orientation.

Finally, in the Chinese parable, the two figures both
make a gesture and speak a *creative* word, not a defiant or
submissive yes or no. In the context here, it shows that men
need to say a clear and decisive yes to the *anima* within, and
to let the feminine side in them be more fulfilled. Women on
the other hand need to say no to many submissive

stereotypes, and not be attracted to male arguments of reason and logic. They need to keep the *animus* within its real bounds, not suppressing it, but setting it recognisable boundaries guided by feminine principles. As creation came into being by the word, so we too become creative by the word we speak upon it.

There is one more facet to the shadow. The shadow is only visible because there is light. And at the deepest and most hidden part of ourselves there is light. The light of Christ is within us. Our journey of listening and awareness does not lead us to ever darker and murkier depths – that is only incidental – but our journey is to the light. On the mountain *top* and in the *deepest* part of the soul there is light.

Some people may find it difficult to apply the term 'soul' to these aspects of the inner being. We have become used to seeing life as different parts, and often they do not meet. Indeed, some people will find it difficult to pray from within a soul which is full of chaos. Yet the psalmist – as so often – puts it succinctly: 'You read my thoughts from far away, whether I walk or lie down, you are watching, you now every detail of my conduct' (Ps. 139:2–3)

## Emotions

As soon as we look into ourselves we encounter great masses of emotions. In pictorial terms we see this often as a sea, a swamp, valleys, or deep wells full of living forces which we cannot quite tackle. As persons we only take up so many square feet of space, yet our inner life can cover miles, both in expanse and in depth.

Sometimes people – especially Christians – think that if they can love enough, all will be well. They put on a brave face and a smile, and for a bit all goes well. Until some event comes along which rocks their security. Then they think they have not loved enough, and try harder, and the smile becomes harder too, and more set. What they are doing is not loving, but deceiving themselves and refusing to listen to what is actually happening.

The effort to love is real, that is for sure. But as soon as we take one strong feeling or emotion seriously, then we will inevitably meet with its opposite. When we dare to listen to all that goes on inside us we meet these forces. We meet them very likely all tangled up, and the store is in a chaotic mess. Love and hate, passions, selfishness, compassion, fury, tenderness, envy, elation, bitterness, hopelessness, excitement, depression, energy, frustration, hope, madness, irritation, cheerfulness – the list can be endless. And each one of us has our own pet emotions which we recognise without having to go searching for them. This is the raw material of our personality, and the ground out of which we speak that creative word. Here too the command is to 'conquer' these emotions (Gen. 1:28). They will tempt us. By listening to them – but *listening* to them, not arguing with them – we can speak that creative word to them which puts them in their rightful place. Because many, or perhaps most of us, have not learnt from childhood onwards how to use our emotions to advantage, we are often afraid of them. We think that they will run away with us. And they often do. The reality and the danger of the shadow is that 'before one has time to think, the evil remark pops out, the plot is hatched, the wrong decision is made and one is confronted with results that were never intended or consciously wanted'.[6] We had not learnt how to use these forces constructively. They are like unschooled children, or like unbroken horses. In their own environment they are legitimate, but not when they are in 'adult' society.

Cathy had always had difficulty in coping with her in-laws. She felt jealous and unloving towards them. She wanted to look at these issues, and consciously set herself targets. A breakthrough came for her when she felt that God was asking her to love herself more. Soon afterwards she had a dream when a big bear came up to her and laid its head on her lap. She could see that loving herself more allowed the bear (the jealousy) to be submitting to her and co-operating with her. She ocould say the creative no to jealousy because she had said the creative yes to herself.

Emotions and feelings tell us what kind of person we are. We are not exclusively good, or loving, or bad, or bitter. We are some of each. The more alive we are, the stronger are also the emotions within us. A person who is asleep emotionally, will not know the difference between a wedding party and a funeral. 'We played the pipes for you, and you wouldn't dance. We sang dirges, and you wouldn't be mourners' (Matt. 11:17). When we are awake, then we are also more 'emotional': aware of the emotions, and using them, glad of their existence.

## Fears

Perhaps the strongest emotion is fear. Roosevelt is supposed to have said that 'the only thing we have to fear is fear itself'. Fear creates fear, and a spiral of fear leads to irrational behaviours. With fear we are out of control, and that is both frightening and creates more fear.

When we listen to ourselves and our inner goings on and encounter this mass of unclear, entangled, yet very strong feelings, we should not be surprised to find ourselves frightened. The fears which we might have to examine are many and varied. Faced with a particular difficulty, the mind normally leaps to 'the worst'. We have indigestion, and fear that really it is a heart attack. We hear an alarm bell go off in the building, and we fear being trapped inside it. We might have to have an operation, and we are convinced that it will turn out to be cancer, and cancer means death. I guess that most of us fear for our survival; we fear death.

Death is the great unknown, and the end of all that we stood for. It is 'the undiscover'd country from whose bourn no traveller returns' (Shakespeare). Yet we know we all have to go there one day.

The inscriptions on some of the gravestones in my local cemetery show clearly how in one way we avoid death even when it is present: 'Passed away'; 'Fell asleep'; 'Gone but not forgotten'. We do everything to avoid death, or to hide it. We spend much time and money on exercises, healthy food, medication, make-up and clothes to avoid illness, old age and death. Sometimes when I see not-so-young joggers

panting around the streets I feel I would like to ask them if
they might spend the amount of time used for running in
sitting down and listening to their souls, asking themselves
what they are running away from.

A young mother who had fought against cancer for many
years was getting more pain. Once again she went to the
hospital, and after examining her, the doctor suggested that
the time had come for her to have some chemotherapy. She
declined, having seen many fellow-patients' severe reactions. She felt sure she had done the right thing, adding 'Of
course if I got really ill then I would have anything.'

Many Christians say that they are not afraid of death.
They are convinced of a better life after death. Indeed, that
is what faith is about. But to come to that faith we need to
go through many processes of fear and doubting. There is a
saying, 'When you meet a man who says he does not fear
death, fear him'. We need to confront ourselves, and fear,
and death. Each has to teach us a great deal. When we do
this confronting in a loving and truthful way, then can we
come to real faith in life. Heschel says that 'Love and truth
are the two ways that lead the soul out of the inner jungle.
Love offers an answer to the question how to think'.[7]
Listening to our fear of death is a means of getting to grips
with who we are.

While fear of death and danger to survival is indeed very
strong in most of us, so is also a fear of danger to self-regard
or self-esteem. When we are not taken seriously, belittled,
pushed aside, disregarded and ridiculed then our need to be
heard has not been met. And who does not know that
feeling! We are afraid to be the failure that we are made to
feel, and we are afraid to be in situations when we might
indeed fail, such as exams, interviews, and situations of any
kind where we have to 'perform'. To avoid defeat we
probably over-compensate. We appear too self-assured, too
cocky, too clever. And then we can't live it down. We are on
that spiral of incompetence leading to more incompetence.
If and when we listen to the incompetence and the fear, we
meet the need to be esteemed. Do we also esteem ourselves?
Can we do that? Do we have enough faith and trust in

ourselves to think highly of ourselves, respect ourselves? Can we do this for the love of God, who loves us? Love and truth are the key to liberating the soul from our inner jungle here too.

Robert was nearing his thirtieth birthday. He was then having repeated dreams of having to go to a doctor and there be examined on his genital area. He was very afraid of this examination and begged the doctor to be gentle with him. Robert had been brought up in a loving home where sexual morality was particularly stressed. This had finally made him inhibited and afraid of anything to do with sexuality. He began to think that he was undeveloped, incapable of love, and not sure if at his age he would ever be taken seriously.

In working with him it was important first to stress all that was good, positive and strong about him. Robert needed to learn to esteem himself and be gentle with his own nature. It took quite a long time before he could bring himself to give a friend a hug and not be afraid.

Another type of fear is that of conflict over enforced dependency, or an irritation over enforced submission. Any of us who have anything to do with institutions will know this fear well. But we know it also in our families. We are given a place, and we are kept in it very firmly. We fear that we may never break through the mould, that we can never be ourselves, and that we can never do it 'my way'.

The shadow within us has probably tried to deal with both the fear and the unsuccessful results of trying to fulfil the need. But the shadow dealt with it in a shadowy way which may be childish, effeminate or brutal, but not 'adult'. Taking time, listening, hearing, being considerate, not condemning but loving, including rather than excluding – all these, and many more things, will help us to see these fears for what they are. They have potential for construction and destruction. Which do we hear?

## Sin and Evil

The springcleaning which heralded the permissive society

was not a bad thing. But as so often, we throw things away in the frenzy of tidying up which we regret only a little while later.

In the clearing up of recent times out went many of the familiar saints, much paternalistic authority, and out went sin and the confession boxes. When the word sin is mentioned today, people feel somewhat uncomfortable, because we don't know it as such any more. By giving it other names we hoped somehow that it would go away. But it hasn't, and because it now has no firm and recognisable name, it is much more difficult to tackle. The bitter pill still has to be swallowed, and making believe that it really is a smartie is not helpful.

Sin has been described in elaborate terms and in simple terms. Lists have been made of what is each kind of sin. Others have said that sin is the opposite of love. It is certainly a deliberate going against that which we know to be right or good. It is offending against God, others, or ourselves. Within that broad framework we have myriads of ways of carrying out a sin.

Marilyn was a devout person, often asking for special prayers for herself. She had difficulties in keeping jobs, blaming them for her inability to do God's will. She always looked for opportunities to do that will, but when they presented themselves she did not follow them. She felt that she was weak and helpless. In fact she was very strong: in pride – to do as *she* wanted; and in self-will because she was able to sustain the game of deceiving herself, those from whom she asked for help, and God.

Recognising our own sin and sinfulness is the beginning of a truly Christian life. Between what we are now and what we are called to become is that time of grace in which we are to be fruitful, and to conquer. The fruits which we are called to produce are 'love, joy, peace, patience, kindness, goodness, trustfulness, gentleness, self-control' (Gal. 5:22–23). Sin is more than the shadow, and stronger than the emotions. When we confront sin we confront not anything unknown, or unconscious, or uncontrollable. We confront our own nature. As we are striving to find our own

particular goal, meaning, or 'word' in life, so we also have
to encounter the opposite, the shadow, of each of these
aspects. The beginning of the Christian life is indeed when
we recognise sin.

Evil is perhaps more dangerous than sin. Evil can be a
force which is greater than ourselves and more pervasive.
We can come into its grip without being aware of it. We see
this particularly in situations like the Nazi era in Germany.
One man's sin becomes such a force that it gets a foothold
in the most unlikely places. There must have been many
people in Germany at that time who genuinely had no idea
what they were doing. Evil can take over and come into the
collective unconscious and there take possession.

In my experience there is always a sense of destructive-
ness and annihilation connected with evil. This can be very
subtle and since evil is an emotive word, not many people
recognise clearly what is happening. I believe that we can
only counter evil with absolute love and compassion: God's
love, and the love of Christ on the cross. If we are not (yet)
strong enough to do that, then we must be very careful with
evil and avoid it altogether when we meet it.

The dividing line, as so often, between good and evil, and
between selfishness and true self-love is very thin. Sometimes we recognise it, and sometimes we don't. But I
believe that to become real people we have to experience
both sides. By avoiding sin and evil we are also avoiding the
experience of forgiveness. St Isaac said that 'he who has
seen his sin is greater than he who has seen the angels'. And
Jourard said that 'the more suffering, enjoying, sinning,
being afraid, becoming psychotic and recovering, being
sick, reading books, having babies, fighting and arguing,
loving and making up, daydreaming you do – in short,
living and learning about yourself – the more you move
toward general practice' (meaning an all-round person).[8]

I am not saying that we *should* sin, and deliberately injure
God's love. But I am saying that when we have sinned and
done wrong, that we then recognise it, become conscious of
it, let it speak to us, and hear what is the necessary step to
take.

One of the things which has got thrown out in the springclean of recent years is the nightly 'examination of conscience'. This has made a return in the form of an 'examen of consciousness': we hear the sin, we become conscious of it but we don't enter into an argument with it. We hear it and then let it go in forgiveness. Like Christ, we have to live through our own wilderness of temptation. When we allow ourselves to do that, then we are also ready to go with Christ to the cross, that ultimate place of fear and death, and there lay our 'burden of sinfulness'.

## Forgiveness and Joy

I venture to say that we cannot experience forgiveness without the experience of sin. Forgiveness is not something which comes cheap. The experience of true forgiveness changes our lives. It may be that point, that experience, which gives meaning to our lives, or which is the catalyst for a personal meaning to emerge. Most of the stories we hear of people witnessing are stories of forgiveness. One of the best known and most dramatic is Paul's experience on the road to Damascus (Acts 9:3–19). Like sin, forgiveness is an intensely personal event. But it is also a collective event. Just as we are all part of human sin and suffering, so we are part of the forgiveness for all humanity. This can be very comforting and make the cross and all its shame not just a stick which threatens us, but the real symbol of transformation.

Many people today find it much easier to accept the stick and see themselves as bad, worthless, and unacceptable. They would however not go all the way and describe themselves as sinners. We find every excuse possible for being worthless and useless, but will not find the excuse, or the reason, within ourselves. I believe that it is largely for this reason that people have the same difficulty in accepting forgiveness. Accepting sin and accepting forgiveness requires us to be truly alive, and most people prefer not to face the stark reality too closely.

Forgiveness is not something which we can earn. This is

perhaps another reason why people shy away from it. They think that they don't deserve it. Our materialistic world has led us to believe that for everything there is a price to pay, and the more it costs, the more it is worth. Forgiveness does not work in this way.

In the realm of faith we cannot apply the same language as in business. Perhaps one of the things which we must learn to hear is that reason is not applicable in the realm of the soul. We cherish reason so much, and measure our performance by it. Here it is impotent; but it is *reason* which is impotent, not we. And how often we confuse the two things!

Derek had been the minister in a lively church. But over a time the sparkle had gone out of the place. Criticism and ostracism had crept in. People wondered what was happening. Derek insisted on his authority and interfered in seemingly trivial matters. Public meetings became vitriolic. At one such meeting a person burst out in anger, saying to the minister, 'I can't bear this any more, I feel like a leper here to be shunned and got rid of'. Stunned silence descended on the meeting. Then Derek shifted uneasily in his chair and with a broken voice haltingly began to say, 'I am the leper. I have leukaemia and to pretend I haven't is killing me'.

Derek admitted that he had been wrong in hiding this fact from his parishioners. He admitted to having been too proud in trying to cope by himself, and also that he was scared of dying, and as a Christian – and a minister at that – he should feel differently. The release of tension in the church and in the various people was the evidence of forgiveness. Healing was then possible in the most unexpected ways.

Like nothing else, forgiveness gives us a sense of release and relief, and in so doing facilitates our listening. It is not something extraordinary and unusual. It is always there. But it has to meet us afresh at all the relevant points in our lives.

The pain in many people today is that they feel worthless. For that reason they cannot accept forgiveness.

How can something so good be given to someone so bad? With forgiveness we have to put reason aside. A person who has received forgiveness is a changed person. Pride, hardness of heart and resistance are turned into repentance, humility, contrition and sorrow. But more than these even the person who is forgiven experiences joy. 'Those who went sowing in tears now sing as they reap' (Ps. 126:5). Forgiveness is liberation, and that gives us the freedom and glory of the children of God (Romans 8:21).

## Creativity and Potential

The experience of forgiveness is often enough to galvanise us into doing and being something which we had never thought possible. It releases in us forces which we had never known. Paul had been a hard-working young Pharisee (Ph. 3:5) but what he was able to achieve after his conversion is quite phenomenal.

Through listening to ourselves, body, environment and soul, we really hear what we are. Hearing makes us not only aware of our unfulfilled needs, and our sins and emotions. It makes us also aware of our strengths. In my counselling work I see again and again how people are changed when they have come to an insight and experienced release through that. This is often described as an 'Aha! experience'. I like to call it an 'I see! experience'. We see with the inner eye, and we see a way ahead, different from the one so far.

Daphne had felt for many years that her mother was standing in her way to full development. She depended on her mother – or rather on her car, her washing machine, her Sunday lunch, and many other 'services' – for her survival. But when they were together they fought. When Daphne stopped and listened to what was happening she could see that she had much to be thankful for. Instead of resenting having to use yet again her mother's lawnmower and be given yet another supper, she was thankful for it. She began to be grateful for all that she was given so freely. This freed her not only from resentment, but made it possible for her to lead a contented life, in turn helping many people around her.

The potential and the meaning of our lives is not to possess something, but to give. One of the sins of our age in particular is that we always want to have more. We are greedy and never satisfied. Not just for more goods – keeping up with the Joneses – but possessing ourselves and each other. We measure ourselves by how much we have. But this is not creative. We waste energy in collecting rather than using energy to create.

We need to grow as persons. We need to accumulate personhood. We need to feel secure. The paradox here is that we can only grow in so far as we sacrifice ourselves. We can only 'become' in so far as we sacrifice that becoming. I am sure that we know all these things, and that we believe them. But to actually experience them is quite different. When we give ourselves the permission to listen to ourselves, then we begin to 'hear' what some of these things mean.

To suddenly find that real person, often cowering under years of inhibitions and censure, is very exciting. It is usually nothing else but fear which leads people to keep themselves locked and hidden. It is fear that we would find there nothing but monsters and wild beasts. When we dare to look inside our souls and look these beasts in the eye, we always find a beautiful person. We always imagine the worst! Trusting in ourselves and our potential is also trusting God. 'Fear is driven out by perfect love' (1 John 4:18) and God is perfect love. Our potential is to become like God: creating love.

## Resistance and Failure

We would not be human if we did not occasionally resist! All this searching, listening, looking, hearing, tasting, smelling and touching of the inside is at times rather wearisome. I have said myself, and I have heard plenty of people say, 'Stop, I have had enough of this'. Life would be much easier without this relentless search in ourselves.

There is a difference between a legitimate pause and a real resistance. A pause to rest may be a need, but a resistance is one of those wants which tends to be selfish. Just as we have a need to sleep in between periods of wakefulness, so we have a need to pause emotionally. Once we have started on a search of ourselves for finding the meaning, or the will of God, we have laid our hand on the plough (Luke 9:62), and to look back is 'copping out'.

We are not made of steel, but flesh and blood. Some of this 'flesh' has its own reason and meaning for resisting. It will always be interested in keeping the easy option alive, in staying in bed, giving in, listening to the voice of reason, not going up to the mountain-top but being content with the view from half-way up. We can call this resistance or temptation, or giving in. Whatever name we give it, we know full well what it is for each of us.

Trying to live a Christian life is often like walking a tightrope between holding on and letting go. Too much holding on or too much letting go, and we are in danger of losing the perspective.

It is often said that when patients in hospital begin to resist the care which they get, then they are on the way to getting better. This is quite true. There is only so much that we can take lying down, and resistance is a way of showing that we are capable of taking control again. The tension here between taking control and letting go is tangible. On a spiritual and emotional level this is also true.

In looking at failures next I would like to start by making a distinction. I see sin as a willing opposition to God, but failures as a part of learning. When we are more aware of the shadow part of ourselves, then we are more aware of our unfulfilled needs. These needs are there within us, but they are not well enough used or adjusted. When we do come to use them we are often clumsy with them, or we come across to others as childish or unsure or emotional. And then we are not able to cope easily with reactions we get. We are reinforced in the well-known feeling of being useless or inadequate. The spiral is perpetuated and we have gained nothing but pain.

Jo was a gregarious sort of person who took the verse 'be still and know that I am God' (Ps. 46:10) to be a personal call to him. He was going to go the whole hog and pray and meditate for an hour every morning. It lasted for a week. Dejected at his inability he set his stakes lower: half an hour. That lasted a few days and then it became twenty minutes, ten, five. Finally he gave up saying that he would never make a good Christian.

It would have been easy to tell him from the beginning that an hour was too much. Jo's nature was such that he needed to learn for himself. With some help he realised that the morning was not his best time, but that he often had a quarter of an hour after supper and before going out for the evening. He felt more in tune with himself and the world then and wanted to use this time to know God in this setting too. This pattern was realistic and Jo used it profitably.

Failures are indeed painful. How familiar that cry of Paul that he cannot do the good which he wants to, but he does the bad which he doesn't want to do (Romans 7:18–23)! In this situation perhaps more than in any other, we need to learn not to punish and chastise, but to listen, become conscious, and accept. With actual sin we need to turn and repent, but with failure we need to accept. We need to accept ourselves and who and what we are. Then the failures will reveal their secrets to us. We do not learn from them by banishing them. We learn from them by accepting them as part of ourselves, even though the shadowy part. Gradually, when we learn to accept ourselves 'warts and all' we may learn how to handle ourselves. In that sense our failures become perhaps our most cherished teachers.

## Finding Meaning

From all that has so far been said it would seem that rather than meaning, when we listen to ourselves, we find only chaos. We find not the will of God but our own will.

It is not only a human law, but a universal law, that a goal is only arrived at through struggle. Gold is only useful after it has been purified. The world came out of chaos (Gen. 1:2). Israel reached the promised land only by passing through the Red Sea (Exod 14:16–22). We usually reach the other side of a wall by not going round it, over it, under it, or along it, but by finding the door through it.

When we are searching for a meaning in and for our lives, the same law and process applies. We have to see the blocks, the possibilities, the fears, the needs, the wants, the sins: the whole chaos. This is not 'bad'. It is the stuff we are made of; our call is to make that stuff holy. We are called to give God not only what he gave us in the first place, but to give it to him improved to the measure that we are capable of (Matt. 25:14–23). We are given the word and we respond to it with our own creative word.

We do not *create* the meaning of our lives, but we hear it, discover it, respond to it. There is already meaning in all things, and through listening and hearing we come close to that meaning.

The choice is ours to do with what we heard. We can use it, or forget about it and hide it and go to sleep like that lone servant, hiding the talent he had been given (Matt. 25:24–30). How sad; yet that one servant is actually in good company.

So far I have talked of *the* meaning in our lives. It need not only be a single meaning. Indeed, for many people, meaning is either a complexity of things, or a succession of things. The meaning or goal in life when we are 21 may not be the same when we are 41 or 61. But for each change of meaning, or emergence of new meaning, we will have to go through some sort of clarification and purification. The word – the *Logos* or meaning – which we are given to hear, comes to us from God and our response is fulfilling that word, giving it its meaning for us.

His friends knew him as JP. He grew up in a large family, and when he was a child he always robbed his older brothers and sisters to give to the younger ones. His father was a true patriarch and very conservative. So JP joined the young socialists. He became a priest and asked to serve only in the poorest parishes. His life changed when an opportunity presented itself to him to do similar work in Cairo. Without a word of Arabic he found his best companions among the *Zebalin*, the 'dustbin children'. He was not only a good priest but a good carpenter too and this skill enabled him to make boxes and carts for them and their pickings. Illness forced him eventually to leave Cairo and he took up a post as chaplain to a community of enclosed nuns. He shared with them his experiences of these poorest of the poor. When he was no longer able to use his carpentry skills he took up embroidery, and ensured that all his friends had a cushion made by him. He stitched his love and joy for each into them, and that is what his friends remember most about him. JP's story hides many struggles and times of what others saw as depression, and in later years, a sense of uselessness.

At each stage JP questioned deeply what was God's will. This led him through valleys of darkness and aloneness, and he often had long and loud disputes with God. But each time he heard God say, 'my grace is enough for you: my power is at its best in weakness' (2 Cor. 12:9).

This surely is true for everyone. We need to search, battle, listen, be weak, and strong, let go, and discover other vistas. To avoid listening is stunting; to dare to listen makes us men and women fully alive.

## References

1 Nouwen, H. J. M. (1978) *Creative Ministry*. Garden City, NY: Doubleday & Co Inc, p.11
2 Maslow, A. (1970) *Motivation and Personality*. (2nd ed.) New York: Harper & Row.
3 Jung, C. G. (1964) *Man and his Symbols*. London: Picador, p.171.
4 Chetwynd, T. (1982) *A Dictionary of Symbols*. London: Paladin Books, p.30.
5 Johnson, R. A. (1977) *She: understanding feminine psychology*. New York: Harper & Row.
6 Jung, C. G. *op cit.*, p.174.
7 Heschel, A. J. (1973) *A Passion for Truth*. New York: Farrar, Straus and Giroux, p.45.
8 Jourard, S. (1971) *The Transparent Self*. New York: Van Nostrand Reinhold, p.205.

4

# Hearing as Responding

Self-awareness is not an end in itself. We listen in order that we know how to respond. This chapter looks at some responses, some outcomes of awareness.

## Hearing is Responding

If the first instinct is to listen, then the second is to respond. So that we respond correctly we will have had to hear correctly. We do not just listen for the sake of listening. We have to do something to show that we have heard, and we show that by how alive we are to others and to God.

In listening and hearing we go further and further into, and inside. The word goes forth, and like the rain, penetrates into the earth, fertilising it. In responding we go out of, and out to. The word returns to its source via the bread which we are, and make, and give to others. The inward journey of listening and hearing is futile, pointless and even destructive if we are not willing to make the return journey outwards and upwards.

Most of us, I am sure, have met people who are seemingly responding, and who give the impression that they have a call to do the work which they are doing. But it is soon evident that they have not really listened. They 'care' for others, 'help' others, are busy doing this and that good work, but essentially they only care for and help themselves. They are responding merely to a convention which says 'thou shalt do good'. But their doing good is hollow because it is not grounded in that fertile chaos and primeval sea of fear, needs, forgiveness, sin, failures and joys.

When we have done our listening and have come to some insight, then the first reaction is often 'I must change . . . I must do . . .'. We see the way forward by and through active change.

Alison had struggled for years to find her meaning – her 'mountain' – in life. She had changed jobs often, hoping each time life would then be all right. In her words, each time she thought, 'It can't have been the right mountain'. She kept looking and searching, taking yet another job, making a bigger effort and a bigger sacrifice, finding a more difficult mountain. When she realised that *she* was the mountain, the realisation was daunting, scary, but immensely 'right' and reassuring. She needed to look not outwards, but inwards, for a change.

Responding is recognising what is in front, and relating to it accurately, be this with outward action, or inward attitude, or both.

Many experiences of insight are quite unexciting. Because of that they so often go unheeded. These experiences bring us an insight about ourselves, and ask of us a change of and in ourselves. Such an experience may have shown us the obvious, and just because it is so obvious we belittle it. When we really learn how to listen, we will recognise also what is important, and what is not, what is a word spoken to us, and what is merely wishful thinking.

It was suggested earlier (p. 33) that you make notes or start a diary while reading this book, of the thoughts and images which come to your mind. In this last part which concentrates on the response which we make to the listening done, this may be even more helpful. What thoughts, words, images, memories or possibilities have come to your mind so far? Look at your list or read your diary and see if there are any patterns or connections which you can make. When you give yourself space and are open to all possibilities presenting themselves, then you will

begin to see, hear, touch, taste and smell the responses
which you might make as you read on.

## Hearing is Believing

One of the ways in which we respond to what we heard is
first of all by simply believing that we heard right.

Because sometimes what we hear is so obvious, we are
inclined to respond, 'Pardon?'. We don't quite trust our
ears. On the other hand, when something extraordinary is
revealed, we don't trust either. Paul, after his experience on
the road to Damascus was so stunned that he could not eat
or drink (Acts 9:9). Similarly, Ananias, who was sent to
Paul, also said, 'Pardon, Lord, but . . .' (Acts 9:13–14).
Our first reaction in so many situations is 'No'. We don't
trust our ears, and like Thomas (John 20:25), we don't trust
our understanding.

Doing a lot of listening sharpens our perception, and
means that we are able to listen more carefully and more
truly. The more we listen and hear, the more we get
accustomed to hearing the real voice, the real word, and not
just our own and other people's wind and fire and
earthquakes (1 Kings 19:11–12). The voice which we hear
when we listen with care, is always a voice which speaks of
love, and compassion, and forgiveness. 'I am listening.
What is the Lord saying? What God is saying means peace
for his people, for his friends' (Ps. 85:8).

Perhaps because we are not 'men of peace' (Luke 10:6)
and of love at heart, we often find it so much easier to hear
of punishment, and guilt. Lyn had arranged for herself a
day of quiet away from home and work. When she got to
her retreat-place she was restless:

I had come
    expecting judgement,
I had come
    to practise self-denial,
I had come
    to be chastised,

To beat body and soul
    into submission.

Fearfully, I waited
    for the
Awesome Voice of God . . .
    Silence.
Then, at last,
    I let Him
Speak to me.

First – a feeling
    in my hands,
As if they were so
    gently held,
Caressed and warmed –
Then, within myself
    the whisper came . . .
  'I love you'
    and again –
  'I love you'.

Slow to understand
  I waited for the
    'But . . .
It did not come –
  Just – 'I love you'
And a plea that
  I may learn
    to love myself.

'And is this all dear Lord?'
    I said
  'It is enough.'
    He said –
  'Love is enough'

And I
    was 'fed'.[1]

When we listen to what goes on in and around us, we become aware of two things: we have to believe in the process of listening itself, and we have to believe what we hear. When we listen, like Lyn in her poem, we have to trust that what we hear is good, and is for our good. The more we listen, the more are we able to trust God to speak peace and love to us.

Is there something in the words or images which you had noticed which you might have to take seriously? It may be that one of them feels somewhat uncomfortable. Why do you think this is? Take it more seriously, and perhaps try to feel – like Lyn felt her hands held – what this is about. It is probably a truth about yourself. Stay with it for a moment, even though it may be uncomfortable. Try to hear what God is saying through it to you, His friend. Make a note of your final thought.

## Hearing is Creating

Listening and hearing are intrinsic parts of the environment for creative living. But they are different for each person.

Hearing is creative on three levels. It is creating the right environment for more and deeper and more accurate listening. It is nurturing and supporting what has already been heard; and it is creating the now, the potential, that which lies hidden within but is waiting to be awakened.

I am again and again surprised by how important preparation is for any task. Perhaps I should not be surprised! We need preparation for cooking, otherwise we find some vital ingredient missing; for a journey otherwise we will have left the most important thing behind; for prayer, otherwise our minds and bodies are in different places; and for listening. We need to prepare the environment so that the task will be successful. We cannot just scatter seeds around and expect them to grow anywhere. They need to be in the right soil, at the right time and under the right conditions.

From the list of words, images, thoughts and possibilities

which you have made, take the word which speaks to you particularly. It need not be the most obvious or most difficult – just the one which attracts you most. Repeat the word slowly a few times. Perhaps form the word into a question, or a prayer.

Now think what you might have to do or be for that word to become 'fruitful'. Do you have to do something? Do you have to speak to someone? What do you have to say? What might you have to listen to? It might be helpful to write some of these things down in diagram or flow chart fashion.

This may not be a big or life-changing decision, but do take it seriously. It is only by taking small steps that we learn to walk, and in practising that we become masters.

We are aware these days of stress and burn-out and tensions at every level. A simple definition of stress is a pulling apart of body and soul. When they don't function in harmony any more then they destroy each other in their quest to get satisfaction. At such a time we need special support and attention.

At a time of hearing how literally, to 'keep body and soul together' because we have done a lot of searching, we need support. We need nurturing, caring, encouraging. We need all the things which help us grow. For some people these are practical things like books and music and enjoyment because these thngs may have been lacking. For other people they may be special friendships and supportive relationships. It may be a soul friend, a prayer partner or a spiritual director who can be particularly helpful. But it needs to be a person who has only our good in mind, and who can guide and strengthen that which has been heard and perceived, and which is growing.

You may need help for the task you have chosen. Who might give the necessary help and support? You may want to think of a few people and what each could give you or help you with. Many people think that they should be self-reliant. If they are not strong in their Christian life then they see it as a failure. But we can think of Jesus who had twelve special companions. We can guess that He got much support from them, from some of them in particular. Some of the others may have been a challenge to Him for clearer thinking and deeper understanding.

Do you need your support person to be nurturing, challenging, guiding, leading? Let yourself be challenged in choosing the one who seems most appropriate at this moment.

The last activity for creative living is seeing the potential and actively nurturing it. When we recognise within ourselves the beginnings of a call or a vocation, or a sense of meaning, we should look at it. When we have had some experience which leads us to stop and think, we should do just that: stop and think. When anything has come at us – helpful or unhelpful – we need to absorb it and let it speak to us. Its message will be pointing to something further, greater. Hunches, dreams, remarks – anything can show us a direction and make us aware of the potential within of the word which seeks an echo; of the rain which does not return without watering and fertilising.

We are called to be creators with God, because we are like Him, His image and likeness (Gen. 1:27). The most immediate and holy thing to do is to be so creative in and of ourselves that others can grow. St Seraphim of Sarov said, 'Acquire inward peace and a multitude of men around you will find their salvation'.[2]

Let your imagination wander and envisage where you might be creative. Where might this present challenge lead to? If you see a possibility stay with it, and by thankful for the opportunity. If you don't see a particular way forward, try to remain open for any other insight or prompting. Both are equally good and equally demanding of faith and hope and love.

You may like to form your thoughts into a short prayer which you can easily remember and repeat during the day. Examples may be:

> Lord, open my eyes that I may see.
>
> Lord, reveal yourself.
>
> My soul magnifies the Lord.

## Hearing is Choosing

In the exercises you have done so far you have made a choice. It may not be the final one, but even to start on a journey of responding to God is a choice. So that we can choose we have to have looked at a number of alternatives, or aspects of the same. When we make a choice we do so with eyes open, and knowing what we are leaving aside. We have to be awake and alert to make a choice, otherwise it is not a choice, only a drifting into something of which we possibly don't even know the name.

One of the hallmarks of choice is that it is made freely. God always gives choice, and when we listen, we know which to choose: 'I set before you life or death, blessing or curse. Choose life, then, so that you and your descendants may live' (Deut. 30:19). We have the choice; it is a precious gift, and we need to treat it accordingly. If we applied pressure, we would never feel satisfied; it would only lead to failure and guilt.

If and when we make a choice we should do it with care, with love and with joy. There is no particular virtue in making a choice with a sour face. We cannot accept to be cross-bearers with a grudge.

Edna had been a nun in a convent but felt that God had asked her to leave the convent. After years outside she still lived like a nun in her observances, but had become a bitter person, telling everyone she met that it was God's will that she left the convent.

When we make a choice, we have to accept the responsibility for it. Edna blamed God, because accepting responsibility for a mistake is not easy. When we recognise our responsibility then the choice we have made liberates us and makes us free truly to be and to become what we have chosen to be.

Many people say that they would like to do the will of God. They then sit back and think it will fall into their lap. When it doesn't happen they think that God is not just, or caring; or that they are not good enough for Him. God will show us His will quite clearly when we listen, respond, and

create the environment: in other words, working actively
with God. By sitting back, the soil does not get prepared,
there is no seed available, and no harvest.

## Hearing is Obedience

In Hebrew, the words for hearing and obedience have the
same grammatical root. There is a sense in which obedience even comes before hearing. When Moses ratified the
covenant between God and the people of Israel, the people
said, 'We will observe all that the Lord has decreed; we will
listen' (Exod. 24:7). It sounds as if it should be the other
way round. But the essence of obedience is that *a priori* it
comes first.

Obedience and commitment go together. When we are
committed to something we identify with it; we are a part of
it. The next step after making a choice is that we prize what
we have chosen. We treasure and savour it. We use it, tell
people about it, and are proud of it. And in so doing we
hear more and more what the meaning of it is for us.

In the choice which you have made of something to
which you would like to pay more attention, where does
obedience come in? What does obedience even mean for
you? Might it mean regular prayer, or staying with the
person you have chosen as supporter even though you don't
always agree? Might it mean that you behave differently in
some circles because of your choice?

You may like to add the words, thoughts or concepts in
connection with obedience to your diary, list or flow chart.
You may like to write some difficult areas about obedience
on a small piece of paper and keep that on your desk, the
fridge door, or by your bed so that you see it frequently for a
time. In this way you become more familiar with such
words and understand what they mean.

When we are obedient we enter a covenant, rather than a
contract. A contract has quite clear limits with rights and
duties set out for both parties. A covenant implies wider
commitment than a contract. The people of Israel entered
not into a contract with God, but a covenant. This did

contain laws and prescriptions, as in a contract, which were
to be kept. People were severely punished if and when they
did not keep those laws. 'My people are diseased through
their disloyalty; they call on Baal, but he does not cure
them. Ephraim, how could I part with you? Israel, how
could I give you up?' (Hos. 11:7–8). The love which God
has for His people is stronger than any wrong-doing, or any
infringement of a contract. He says 'I am God, not man'
(Hos. 11:9). The covenant of hearing which we enter with
our choice demands of us that we are obedient to the voice
of the covenant.

## Hearing is Self-Discipline

The response which we make to all that we listened to
characterises us as persons. We shall be known by our fruits
(Matt. 7:20).

Like humility, sin, or chastity, self-discipline is not a
word which rolls easily off the tongue these days. These
words have become old-fashioned. But their reality has not
changed. Whatever name we give to self-discipline, the fact
of it remains. We gain that freedom and peace which comes
with a meaningful and fulfilled life only when we have
learnt and accepted that self-discipline is a part of it.

Self-disclipline is not gritting our teeth; it is not making
ourselves of steel and saying 'No' each time we meet
something good or desirable. Self-discipline, as in the
parable of the Chinese man and woman, is saying a *creative*
yes and a *creative* no in the right place and at the right time.
Self-discipline is the art of seeing all the good things and all
the negative things, and choosing to go the way which is
creative.

This may mean giving up something which would have
been useful and helpful. In biblical terms it means offering
the other cheek, giving the cloak as well as the tunic, and
going two miles instead of only one (Matt. 5:39–42).

What does self-discipline mean for you? In the light of
the choices made so far, where does self-discipline fit in? Do
you have to be more generous with time and talents? Do
you have to be less rigid in your judgements?

Self-discipline starts today, not tomorrow. What will you have to do today (and carry on doing) so that your life is made more whole, creative, holy?

The art of self-discipline is in how we use power. As with so many things which we have looked at, and listened to, power has its positive and negative sides. We can use it for construction or destruction. Self-discipline implies that we are positive, and constructive and creative. We decide to be positive, and we stick to it. And sticking to it is sometimes great and uplifting, and sometimes it seems nothing but trouble, and most of the time it is just an ordinary plodding on and not giving in; a sticking with it even though there is no immediate result. Self-discipline *is* denial, renunciation, sacrifice, detachment, suffering. But it is that power which leads us beyond ourselves. It is that rain which waters the earth and makes it fertile to bring forth bread. And it is bread which becomes sacrament, becomes body, to be given for others.

### Hearing is Celebrating

When we are aware and awake, we are aware of who we are, what we are, and what our powers are and how we use them. This gives us freedom.

Self-discipline gives us freedom. We are no longer under a yoke of forces which we are afraid of and which torment us. The essence of self-discipline is that it goes on. As if to keep the flame of self-discipline alive, events are given us for celebrating. When we become quite sure of our own ground then the discipline can be relaxed sometimes. But we have to feel good about it. We need to use our power to give ourselves the permission, and we don't feel guilty about it. We can really enjoy it. And to celebrate we have to be awake. Those who are afraid to be awake are also afraid to celebrate.

We need to celebrate big events and little events. We need to celebrate with others and alone. We need to celebrate getting and letting go. In the search of finding meaning in life we have to listen to all the events which surround us, and festivals and celebrations of all kinds are high spots. There is a lot of pain and suffering in life, and so as not to forget it, but to put pain and suffering into perspective, we celebrate. But how often we take things for granted! Finding a sheep or a coin (Luke 5:4–10) hardly touches us, let alone excites us. To be able to celebrate we have to be awake, and to be inspired.

Celebration is not just a glass of champagne. It is that very often – but celebrating is holding the object close, looking at it, cherishing it, enthusing over it. We do this quite easily with something tangible, like a new car, or a piece jewellery. We are not so often in the habit of doing it with some insight, or a spiritual experience, or a word understood.

What might you have to celebrate now?

If you have come to an insight and made a choice, this is cause for celebration. Did you thank God for the inspiration? Did you tell your supporter that because of his or her help you are now more sure again of God's love? You may need or want to tell other people of your insight, and in doing so it will become more real and tangible for you. This may be your celebration. You may also, like the woman in the parable, invite your friends for a meal and celebrate with them the beginning of a new adventure for you – an adventure to follow more closely the call of God. Or you may want to make a contribution in time or money to some particular cause which is relevant at this moment.

Decide what your celebration might be, and carry it out.

We can only truly celebrate when we understand what meaning life and death, beginning and end have. Here we have once more that same paradox of having to start backwards: we obey and we hear. Celebrating does not only come after the event. Unless we are willing first of all to enter into life and death and celebrate them, we will never hear what they are about.

We celebrate because the object of our joy is transitory. A coin is easily lost. A friend is easily gone. A word heard spoken is only a 'gentle breeze'. So when we 'have' them we have to celebrate to give them their value. We sometimes say that we have to pinch ourselves to believe that something is true. Everything that is given us is true, and celebrating is that pinching: making sure that it is there.

There is a sense in which we also have to remember before we can celebrate. The celebration of sins forgiven, of the prodigal son returning home (Luke 15:11–32), a reconciliation – all these require that we remember something in the past which is now different. We remember the Lord's suffering and death and resurrection, and that is cause for celebration every week, every day.

By remembering things from the past and celebrating them now, we affirm the future. I have on a number of occasions experienced how losing one friend through death, has meant making more friends through meeting their families. Death is indeed swallowed up in victory (1 Cor. 15:54). But the death had to happen; there is no victory without it.

## Hearing is Acting

When we listen we become aware of our bodies, our surroundings, our souls, our relationships, our actions and the influences which we have. We become aware of ourselves in order to lose ourselves. We become aware of ourselves in order to transcend ourselves. We become doers of the word, not only listeners (James 1:22). Through listening we have heard our call and meaning in life; now we need to put it into practice.

As we search for what these actions might be, we have an example and a rich choice: 'To bring good news to the poor, to proclaim liberty to captives and to the blind new sight, to set the downtrodden free, and to proclaim the Lord's year of favour' (Luke 14:18–19; Isa. 35:5–6; 42:6–7; 49:9).

As Christians we are specifically called to follow our Lord and to do the works which He did, and to do even greater works (John 14:12). When we listen to what goes on around us we hear of hunger in body and mind; thirsting of souls for forgiveness; sick people who are imprisoned in their own minds or houses; blindness to social issues – in short we are all of us captive in some way and need to hear of liberty, and of captivity being made captive (Ps. 68:18).

Is there in this list of actions one which is specifically for you? Do you find there your job description? Have you been doing one of these works already? Does it need to be refreshed? Ask yourself seriously what your response should be. It may be that you don't need to 'do' or 'change' anything, but be or become more grateful for what you are doing, and the gifts you have been given already. Sometimes we overlook the need to celebrate our gifts and be thankful for them.

I remember the postmaster in a small village who seemed to be the unofficial counsellor simply by the way he greeted his customers. His 'How are you today?' drew people as much to him as to his stamps. Or the nurse who had that knack of arranging the pillows in such a way that the patients always slept well.

What we hear within ourselves will determine the response which we make. When we have listened to other people we will have heard their needs, and we respond. Our call, our meaning in life, manifests itself in the way we care for others and all creation.

Ware quotes an interesting story from the Desert Fathers: 'A monk told Abba Poemen, "Some brethren have come to live with me; do you want me to give them orders?" "No", said the Old Man. "But Father", the monk persisted, "they themselves want me to give them orders." "No", repeated Poemen, "be an example to them but not a lawgiver".'[3]

Being a lawgiver gives people no chance to hear themselves. We all like to be told what to do. It is less hassle and less mental effort. Here come the sleepers again! But by our example we help to wake people up.

The first action then, which we can do for others, is not persuading them, or leading them, to where we have come from; it is being an example. And here we come straight back to self-discipline: we have no ground for being any example to anyone if we are not disciplined ourselves first.

In our caring we need to be listening well to what is required of us.

Are you an example? By what do you measure yourself? Do you draw any conclusions from the decisions and choices which you have made?

Some of the works which we do in life change as we go along. Do you need to make a change, or a new start? Take seriously any thoughts and 'words' which your soul speaks to you. Listen to them, hold them, celebrate them, and ask God to show you the way. It may be through an action that you discover what this may mean for you. Do that action, and don't put it off.

An elderly relative of mine, who had raised a large family, spent her last years calling to mind all those whom she knew. She could not 'do' anything more for her family, but she prayed, and very faithfully so. To be in her presence was like being near a warm stove, and her blind eyes shone brightly. She had found her ultimate meaning in life, and her response was total. Her prayer was the 'prayer of the saints' (Rev. 5:8) 'to the glory of God and the good of all his church'.

Prayer and intercession is also a good work, though often done in silence and alone. Interceding for others is a work of love which demands attention, time, and a good deal of tenacity. The story of Moses praying while the people did battle is very poignant. The Israelites only had the upper hand in battle while Moses' arms were outstretched. When he let his arms fall, Israel was losing. So two men had to support Moses' arms, to keep them up (Exod. 17:8–16). Our actions are like battles on the front; our prayers sustaining the actions.

Intercession, the great work of holding people and causes before God, is the link between active 'doing' and 'being' face to face with God (Num. 12:8). Intercession is not just reeling off names; it is holding each one before God. When we care for someone we pray for him or her. Is prayer a part of the meaning of our lives? Prayer is first of all a listening:

to the Word of God in the soul. When prayer is also a response, then will it be like the word which returns to God having fulfilled its mission.

As we listen to everything around us, and deep in our souls, we begin to hear of possible ways of responding, or possible new and different ways. When we believe the words which we hear, then we become bold and can take risks, trying out some forms of action. They may not be immediately the right and best actions, but they will help us to find the right path.

## Hearing is Loving

Every effort which we make is for love. Every good deed which we do is out of love. Every prayer which we are conscious of is in love.

Love is a rather over-worked word. I would like to use it here in its simple form: the basic force in all of us, that which, together with listening, is intrinsic. Listening and loving are like two poles, holding each other in balance. Without the one, the other is unable to function.

We are made in the image and likeness of God (Gen. 1:27), and that God is love (1 John 4:8). God sends His word so that it will come back to Him fulfilled: God listens to what the 'fulfilled' word says to Him. Through listening and loving we are not only doing God's will, but we are *in* God.

The great sin of Adam and Eve was that they had not listened to God (Gen. 3:1–13). Our sin and shortcoming is that too often we don't listen either – neither to ourselves, nor to others, nor to God. But when we do listen, we come back again into that creative force which is loving.

Through listening we become aware of ourselves, we hear ourselves. That is the beginning of loving. The great commandment is that we love God and our neighbour *as ourselves* (Luke 10:27). Listening to ourselves means that we listen to ourselves rightly. Most of us love ourselves too much or too little; we are selfish or feel totally worthless. When we listen to ourselves we hear that we are loved, and can be loving: we believe what we hear. That is the

beginning of wisdom (Ps.111:10). That is also the beginning of being alive to all and everything around us.

What we hear when we listen to ourselves is that we are
God's temple (1 Cor. 3:16). God is not ouside or above, but
within, to the measure that we let Him be so.

Meister Eckhart, the thirteenth-century German mystic
said 'You may call God love, you may call God goodness.
But the best name for God is compassion'.[4] In listening to
others we hear God. In listening to God we recognise
ourselves truly for what we are.

Loving is hearing, and hearing is loving. We have to do a
lot of hearing to begin to understand what loving is about.
But that loving is nothing much to do with sentiment. It is
to do with compassion, forgiveness, and creating.

One of the hallmarks of love is that it never judges or
makes lists of rank and priority. All around us we hear of
wishing for this and that. Competition is the name of the
game. But with love that aspect of life loses its importance.
We have to find our means of expressing love, but one act of
love is not better than another, it is simply different.

Through the listening and praying which you have done
while reading this book, what does love now say to you?
Does it mean anything in particular, or simply more insight
into who you are, and who God is in and for your life? Do
you have to affirm that love in a special way? Perhaps 'love'
is too wide a word and you need to give it a more particular
meaning – what is that meaning? Do you need to put it into
action? What is that action? Can you do it, or start to do it
now?

When we love our neighbour then we also love God.
Giving a cup of cold water (Matt. 10:42) to a little one means
giving it to God (Matt. 25:40). We do not love God whom we
cannot see if we do not love our brothers and sisters whom
we can see (1 John 4:20). Therefore to love God is indeed to
love those who surround us: by proclaiming the good news,
opening outward and inward eyes, visiting those in prisons
of any kind, and enabling the deaf to hear and listen to
themselves, and nature, and God. This is the kind of loving
which is real caring. This kind of loving is, as Campbell